CW0092l209

SMALL *Oxford* BOOKS

HOTELS & INNS

SMALL *Oxford* BOOKS

———————— ❧❧ ————————

HOTELS & INNS

———————— ❧❧ ————————

Compiled by
HILARY RUBINSTEIN

Oxford New York
OXFORD UNIVERSITY PRESS
1984

Oxford University Press, Walton Street, Oxford OX2 6DP

London Glasgow New York Toronto
Delhi Bombay Calcutta Madras Karachi
Kuala Lumpur Singapore Hong Kong Tokyo
Nairobi Dar es Salaam Cape Town
Melbourne Auckland

and associated companies in
Beirut Berlin Ibadan Mexico City Nicosia

Oxford is a trade mark of Oxford University Press

British Library Cataloguing in Publication Data

Hotels and inns.
1. Hotels, tavern, etc
I. Rubinstein, Hilary
647'.94   TX911
ISBN 0-19-214142-2

*

FOR CAROLINE

who shares my hotel watch,

with affection and gratitude

Set by New Western Printing Ltd.
Printed in Great Britain by
Hazell Watson & Viney Limited
Aylesbury, Bucks

Introduction

This book celebrates the hotel in fact and fiction. Hotels and inns have a fascination for some, and bore others. They may be considered as no more than convenient night-stops – places to change horses or catch a coach or fulfil a business engagement. For many, they are a necessary evil, at best offering a decent night's rest and at worst, an occasion for being bitten by bedbugs, kept awake by traffic and roistering neighbours, poisoned, ripped off – or a combination of all these forms of persecution.

But hotels can wear a very different face. They can be houses of blissful assignation and hallowed in memory of honeymoons. We may not find ourselves setting off to Canterbury in the company of mine host of the Tabard Inn, but strange and wonderful experiences can still happen when we travel abroad. And for many of us who spend eleven months of the year at an office desk or factory bench, a weekend at a good hotel is a memorable if short-lived taste of a fantasy life, enriched by exotic meals, flattered by immaculate service, and pampered as no one ever pampers us at home.

My own interest in hotels was quickened when I was hitch-hiking in Ireland, on first coming down from university. A chance encounter brought me to the door of an extraordinary establishment at the remote western end of Achill Island in County Mayo. The house had belonged in the eighteenth century to Captain Boycott – the man who gave his name to that form of embargo – but in 1950 was owned by an eccentric Englishman, Major Freyer. His rank derived from service in the London Artists Rifles in the First World War thirty-five years earlier, where he had been in charge of a clothing depot in London's Olympia, though he had spent his nights drinking in the Café Royal.

I turned up at Achamore House without advance booking, and was met at the door by an attractive young girl named Bridie. I asked for a room, and was told to wait while Bridie went and consulted the Major. I heard later from fellow guests, who were with the Major when I arrived, that he had asked Bridie whether I was an O.M.; this acronym stood for Oldy Mouldy, and characterized the typical hotel guest at more conventional hostelries. When Bridie reported that I didn't look like an O.M., the Major came out and inspected me in person. I was shortly afterwards accommodated in a fine large room, looking out over the sea towards the nearest western land mass, North America.

Achamore House was full of unconventional features. The Major didn't charge you if he didn't think you could afford it, but charged you extra if you didn't have a bath every day. You were under some duress to drink and gossip with him till the early hours, and on Sundays were expected to join in English folk-dancing which he had inaugurated, to the amazement of his Irish neighbours, in an open-air theatre he had built in his grounds.

Rarely, rarely come the Achamore Houses of such delight. But those of us who travel hopefully can still be rewarded beyond our desserts – or at least have pungent experiences on which we can dine out on our return and recall nostalgically in later years, when we have become mouldies ourselves and no longer eligible to enter Major Freyer's elysium.

Certain writers in every age – notable among them Smollett, Dickens, Arnold Bennett, and, in recent times, John Irving, D. M. Thomas, and John (*Fawlty Towers*) Cleese – have responded brilliantly to the comic and dramatic possibilities of the subject. But there are gems to be found, too, in many obscure corners. Every extract in this book could have been duplicated many times, and some of my favourite passages had in the end to be excluded on grounds of length. Bon voyage!

Inns of Happiness

Many writers have written nostalgically about inns, but none as memorably as Hilaire Belloc: even the fleas are recollected wih affection ...

Do you remember an Inn,
Miranda?
Do you remember an Inn?
And the tedding and the spreading
Of the straw for a bedding,
And the fleas that tease in the High Pyrenees,
And the wine that tasted of the tar?
And the cheers and the jeers of the young
    muleteers
(Under the vine of the dark verandah)?
Do you remember an Inn, Miranda,
Do you remember an Inn?
And the cheers and the jeers of the young
    muleteers
Who hadn't got a penny,
And who weren't paying any,
And the hammer at the doors and the Din?
And the Hip! Hop! Hap!
Of the clap
Of the hands to the twirl and the swirl
Of the girl gone chancing,
Glancing,
Dancing,
Backing and advancing,
Snapping of a clapper to the spin
Out and in –
And the Ting, Tong, Tang of the Guitar!
Do you remember an Inn,
Miranda?
Do you remember an Inn!

Never more;
Miranda,
Never more.
Only the high peaks hoar:
And Aragon a torrent at the door.
No sound
In the walls of the Halls where falls
The tread
Of the feet of the dead to the ground
No sound:
But the boom
Of the far Waterfall like Doom.

Hilaire Belloc, 'Tarantella', 1923

A hundred years earlier, in 1820, the American writer Washington Irving recorded his supreme contentment in the parlour of the Red Horse, Stratford-upon-Avon, warming his feet before the fire.

To a homeless man, who has no spot on this wide world which he can truly call his own, there is a momentary feeling of something like independence and territorial consequence, when, after a weary day's travel, he kicks off his boots, thrusts his feet into slippers, and stretches himself before an inn fire. Let the world without go as it may; let kingdoms rise or fall, so long as he has the wherewithal to pay his bill, he is, for the time being, the very monarch of all he surveys. The arm-chair is his throne; the poker his sceptre, and the little parlor of some twelve feet square, his undisputed empire. It is a morsel of certainty, snatched from the midst of the uncertainties of life; it is a sunny moment gleaming out kindly on a cloudy day; and he who has advanced some way on the pilgrimage of existence knows the importance of husbanding even morsels and moments of enjoyment. 'Shall I not take mine ease in mine inn?' thought I, as I gave the fire a stir, lolled back in my elbow chair, and cast a complaisant look about the little parlor of the Red Horse, at Stratford-on-Avon.

Washington Irving, *The Sketch Book of Geoffrey Crayon*, 1820

Here is another tribute, which comes unexpectedly from a 1924 issue of the London Times. *This 'perfect' hotel, which is still in business, is the San Giorgio at Lenno on Lake Como.*

He was not great, his path in life was not glorious – he was indeed of peasant birth. But he had genius – he was the perfect host. From long years ago, when he first soared from waiting to inn-keeping in an Italian lakeside village, he had developed this genius; patiently, with that diligence which was inherited from his thrifty forefathers, who had won their small crops from the rocky steeps about the lake, he garnered each opportunity. The little old inn in the village, with its brown walls and green shutters, its vine-shaded garden tables, was his first big venture. The solid, square pink house by the lake quay with the linden alley in front of it was his second. What memories those walls contain!

For it was here that he first exercised to the full his hostship: here that from afar off, year by year, his circle of guests, his friends, gathered together in increasing numbers to rest, to make merry, or to dream beside the matchless waters: the artists, the players, the poets, and the plain men. Here, too, he gathered round him his family: his handsome wife, his eldest son, the little child whose death threw for so long a shadow, and, last of all, a late-comer, the baby who was his special pride, Giorgio, so called in honour of his English friends. And here his brother and sister, sharers in some measure in his gift, shared loyally in all his labours. And here he hatched, after the weary years of war service, the final scheme, the great ambition – another hotel: perfect, this one, in every detail, with balconies and gardens, with 'running water in every room', with many bathrooms. It was a strange whim of his friends for so much running water in pipes when the lake lay broad before them, but it must be gratified.

And yet when, after incredible difficulties and persistence the perfect hotel was finished he never ceased to urge the claims of the old house by the quay – 'Et is veiry naice', he would say, 'most comfortable and I charge there less – no tax of luxury.' And then with a sigh: 'But here – oh! my hot water! beautiful, beautiful.' The word beautiful was, indeed, the most used in his English vocabulary: for the hot water, for the omelette, for the baby, for the late snows on the mountains all a–sheen beneath the Easter moon. And sometimes he used it tenderly as when he divined a guest in sorrow – a little deserted wife. 'How sad,' he said softly, 'to see her left all young, like a beautiful flower broken and thrown away – never any more to be sheltered, never any more her home – just a beautiful flower she is, so sad –' And he stared out across the lake all solemn in a moment.

But his friends seldom remember him as solemn – rather as vivid, shrewd, sometimes irascible, always

eager to help, to welcome, to make merry, to understand. Whether he was urging a guest to some fresh
delicacy at dinner or swearing down the ever-faulty
telephone, or sitting by his baby on the shore and
teaching him to throw stones into the blue water, he
was always human, vital, part of the landscape. And
now, all too soon, he has gone.

George Herbert pictured an inn of welcome on the
road to heaven. There must be room there yet for our
perfect host. But here we shall not find him again.

A correspondent in *The Times, The Perfect
Host and the Perfect Hotel*, 1924

*When Patrick Leigh-Fermor was walking through
Europe in 1933 he found a true inn of welcome on an
icy December night in Heidelberg.*

It was dark by the time I climbed the main street of
Heidelberg and soon softly-lit panes of coloured glass,
under the hanging sign of a Red Ox, were beckoning
me indoors. With freezing cheeks and hair caked with
snow, I clumped into an entrancing haven of oak
beams and carving and alcoves and changing floor
levels. A jungle of impedimenta encrusted the interior
– mugs and bottles and glasses and antlers – the
innocent accumulation of years, not stage props of
forced conviviality – and the whole place glowed with
a universal patina. It was more like a room in a castle
and, except for a cat asleep in front of the stove, quite
empty.

This was the moment I longed for every day. Settling
at a heavy inn-table, thawing and tingling, with wine,
bread, and cheese handy and my papers, books and
diary all laid out; writing up the day's doings, hunting
for words in the dictionary, drawing, struggling with
verses, or merely subsiding in a vacuous and contented
trance while the snow thawed off my boots. An elderly
woman came downstairs and settled by the stove with
her sewing. Spotting my stick and rucksack and the
puddle of melting snow, she said, with a smile, 'Wer

reitet so spät durch Nacht und Wind?' My German, now fifteen days old, was just up to this: 'Who rides so late through night and wind?' But I was puzzled by *reitet*. (How was I to know that it was the first line of Goethe's famous *Erlkönig*, made more famous still by the music of Schubert?) *What, a foreigner?* I knew what to say at this point, and came in on cue ...'Englischer Student...zu Fuss nach Konstantinopel' ...I'd got it pat by now. 'Konstantinopel?' she said. '*Oh Weh!*' O Woe! So far! And in midwinter too. She asked where I would be the day after, on New Year's Eve. Somewhere on the road, I said. 'You can't go wandering about in the snow on Sylvesterabend!' she answered. 'And where are you staying tonight, pray?' I hadn't thought yet. Her husband had come in a little while before and overheard our exchange. 'Stay with us,' he said. 'You must be our guest.'

They were the owner and his wife and their names were Herr and Frau Spengel. Upstairs, on my hostess's orders, I fished out things to be washed – it was my first laundry since London – and handed them over to the maid: wondering, as I did so, how a German would get on in Oxford if he turned up at the Mitre on a snowy December night.

Patrick Leigh-Fermor, A *Time of Gifts*, 1977

Even the most modest inn can please. Robert Louis Stevenson records his impressions of an auberge in the Cevennes when travelling with his donkey, Modestine.

The *auberge* of Bouchet St Nicolas was among the least pretentious I have ever visited; but I saw many more of the like upon my journey. Indeed, it was typical of these French highlands. Imagine a cottage of two storeys, with a bench before the door; the stable and kitchen in a suite, so that Modestine and I could hear each other dining; furniture of the plainest, earthen floors, a single bed-chamber for travellers, and that without any convenience but beds. In the kitchen

cooking and eating go forward side by side, and the
family sleep at night. Anyone who has a fancy to wash
must do so in public at the common table. The food is
sometimes spare; hard fish and omelette have been my
portion more than once; the wine is of the smallest,
the brandy abominable to man; and the visit of a fat
sow, grouting under the table and rubbing against
your legs, is no impossible accompaniment to dinner.

But the people of the inn, in nine cases out of ten,
show themselves friendly and considerate. As soon as
you cross the doors you cease to be a stranger; and
although this peasantry are rude and forbidding on
the highway, they show a tincture of kind breeding
when you share their hearth. At Bouchet, for instance,
I uncorked my bottle of Beaujolais, and asked the host
to join me. He would take but little.

'I am an amateur of such wine, do you see?' he
said, 'and I am capable of leaving you not enough.'

Robert Louis Stevenson, *Travels with a
Donkey*, 1879

*Sybille Bedford finds her corner of paradise in a
Mexican posada.*

The *posadas* are run by honest, mildly prosperous, commercial Mexicans for other mildly prosperous, commercial Mexicans. The ground floor is always a large,
unkempt parlour opening into the patio without much
transition, full of overgrown plants, wicker-chairs,
objects without visible use; birds free and caged, and a
number of sleeping dogs. Here the innkeepers jot their
accounts, sort the linen, drive bargains with the poultry
woman and the egg child, arraign the servants, play
the gramophone, drink chocolate, chat and doze; and
here the guests sit, smoke cigars, have their hair cut,
shout for servants, play the gramophone, drink rum
and chocolate, chat and doze. Everybody has their own
bottle, sent out for by the *mozo*. The innkeeper would
think you mad to pay him bar prices; every time you
draw cork he will supply you – compliments of the

house – with glasses, limes, salt (without which spirits are considered to be unswallowable), pistachio nuts, fried anchovies, toasted *tortillas* strewn with crumbs of cheese and lettuce, stuffed cold maize dumplings and pickled chilli peppers. The three more substantial meals are taken in the COMIDOR, an uncompromising rectangle marked thus and partitioned off the parlour by a glass door. The bedrooms are very clean, quite bleak and full of beds. There is always plumbing, recent and proudly displayed. The rule is a basin, shower-bath and w.c. right inside the room. There are no screens, and not always a window. In that case one just leaves the door open and soon gets used to it, nobody inside or out ever paying the slightest attention. The service at some hours is zealous and alarmingly imaginative (in one place they unpacked for us and we found every article regardless of use arranged in a symmetrical pattern on the floor); at other hours, early morning, siesta, after dinner, there is no service at all. The terms are something between eight and ten shillings a day for accommodation (the room to yourself if you are alone and the room for seven if you are seven) and all the food you can eat. There are no taxes, no service charges, no extras; that is there *are* extras : errands, coffee, chocolate, drinking water, sweet bread, fruit all day long, but you do not pay for them. Washing is one and sixpence a dozen, whether the dozen be shirts, dresses, flannels, socks or handkerchiefs, and is returned in immaculate condition the same day. Breakfast, around ten o'clock, is ham-and-eggs or eggs-and-chilli, followed by beefsteak with sliced tomatoes, followed by black beans; *tortillas*, rolls, buns, sweet bread and cake; jam, honey and stewed fruit; papayas, muskmelon, bananas and prickly pears; coffee or chocolate. The coffee nowadays is often imported from Guatamala, and very good; the chocolate can be ordered in three different styles, French, Mexican and Spanish. French chocolate is beaten frothy with cream, Mexican is plain thick black, and Spanish is black whipped with cinnamon. Some guests have four eggs, two beefsteaks, three cups of chocolate and an extra basket of sweet bread. Their smaller children sit hoisted on the laps of girl servants – a servant per baby – who hold their mouths open and stuff them with slow conscientiousness course for course like so many little geese. For luncheon there will be a tureen of good soup; then a dish of dry soup; then fish; a baked vegetable; a made *plat de résistance*, sweet peppers stuffed with bean-paste-and-beef, or choyotes with pork-mince-and-curds, or a turkey curry; then a vegetable salad; some scraps of fowl; a green salad; fried mashed beans; a very sweet sweet; stewed fruit; mangoes, papayas, guavas, persimmons, muskmelon, prickly pears and bananas; and of course *tortillas*, bread, sweet bread, cake, coffee and chocolate. Before lunch the men drink rum and Coca-Cola, just before lunch they drink *tequila*, with lunch they drink beer and after lunch coffee and chocolate. The women and children drink Coca-Cola, bottled orange fizz, more bottled orange fizz, and chocolate. Supper in the provinces is at nine, and a shorter meal – chicken broth, omelette, a hot vegetable course, beefsteak or cutlets, a salad, beans, fruit, breads and chocolate, perhaps an extra piece of cake for the children, but you *may* ask for many things that aren't on the table.

Sybille Bedford, *A Visit to Don Otavio.
A Mexican Journey*, 1982

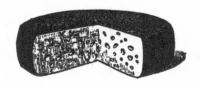

Inns of Iniquity

Fastidious travellers have been complaining about inns – the accommodation, or lack of it, the wretched food, the graceless service – for at least 2,000 years: indeed, 'no room at the inn' has a distinctly modern ring. But of all the plagues that can beset the unlucky guest, it is hard to think of a worse one than was in store for thirteenth-century visitors to the Ostrich at Colnbrook on the old Bath Road.

Foreign ambassadors and other dignitaries on their way to Windsor used the Ostrich a great deal, and King John is said to have stopped here for refreshment on his way to Runnymede to put his seal reluctantly to Magna Carta. Fortunes must have declined by the time Jarman, the villainous innkeeper, began supplementing his income by murdering selected visitors. The bed in the main bedroom stood upon a hinged flap, directly above the inn's brewhouse. When the intended victim was well asleep, the flap would be released and the bed would swing over to drop him into the waiting cauldron of boiling water. It was later estimated that Jarman and his wife disposed of more than fifty unfortunates in this way.

Like many regular killers, they grew careless and too impatient. On three successive occasions they tried to manoeuvre a well-to-do clothier from Reading, Thomas Cole, into that particular bed, but each time were thwarted. On the fourth time that he stayed in the Ostrich on his way to London, all seemed to be going smoothly: Cole was in bed, the fire was burning nicely, the water was bubbling away. But Jarman felt uneasy. He tried to persuade his wife that they ought not to push their luck too far. Mrs Jarman, however, was a

frugal lady and didn't fancy wasting the fuel and the
boiling water. They went ahead; Cole was duly killed,
and his body thrown into the nearby brook. It was
quickly found, the inn was searched, and some of
Cole's belongings were identified. The Jarmans were
hanged.   John Burke, *The English Inn*, 1981

*Officials, soldiers, and pilgrims were using the roads
throughout the Middle Ages, but tourism in the
contemporary sense may be said to have started with
the Renaissance. Erasmus, a Renaissance man* par
excellence, *travelled extensively throughout Europe and
grumbled much about his bed and board. In one of his*
Colloquies, *written in 1523, he writes with particular
venom about the vileness of German inns.*

No one greets the arrival, lest they seem to be on the
lookout for a guest; that they consider base and de-
grading, unworthy of Germanic austerity. When you've
shouted a long time, someone finally sticks his head
out of the little window of the stove room (where
they spend most of their time until midsummer), like a
turtle from his shell. You must ask him if you may
put up there. If he doesn't shake his head, you know
there's room for you. You move into the stove room
with all your impedimenta – leggings, luggage, and
mud. If you want to wash your hands, water is

fetched, but usually it's so dirty that afterwards you
have to look for other water to wash it off with!

They don't prepare anything unless they see everyone's present, in order to serve them all in one
operation. There are often eighty or ninety met
together in the same stove room: travellers on foot,
horsemen, traders, sailors, carriers, farmers, young men,
women, the sick and the whole. One combs his hair,
another wipes the sweat off, another cleans his rawhide
boots or leggings, another belches garlic. You're not
allowed to ask for anything meanwhile. When the
evening's already late and no more arrivals are expected, an aged servant with white beard, cropped
head, grim look, and dirty clothes makes his appearance.
Glancing about, he silently counts the people in the
stove room. The more he sees there, the more ener-
getically he fires up the stove, even though the
weather's oppressively warm without it. Among these
folk it's a principal part of good management to melt
everybody in sweat. If someone not used to steam
should open a window to escape suffocation, he hears
instantly, 'Close it!' If you reply, 'I can't stand this,'
they tell you, 'Then look for another inn.'

After everyone is all seated, our gloomy Ganymede
appears again and counts his company once more.
Sometimes you sit and wait almost an hour. At last
the wine is served – good Lord, anything but mellow!
But if some guest, even offering a tip on the side, asks
them to find him another kind of wine, at first they
ignore him, but looking as if they're about to murder
him. If you press them, they'll reply, 'So many counts
and marquises have stayed here, and not one of them
complained about my wine. If you don't like it, look
for another inn.' Soon afterward, amidst much
ceremony, dishes arrive. The first generally has bits of
bread dipped in meat broth; or, if it's fish day, in bean
juice. Next another broth; after that some warmed-over
meat or salt fish. Again porridge, followed by more
solid food; next they serve to the thoroughly tamed

stomach roast meat or boiled fish – not altogether despicable, but they're stingy with it and quickly take it away. The uproar and tumult after they've all begun to grow heated from drink is astonishing. In short, it's completely deafening. Often jesters mingle with the guests. Despite the fact that no class of men is more detestable, you'd scarcely believe how fond of them the Germans are: they sing, chatter, shout, dance, and stamp, until the stove room seems about to collapse. You can't hear a word anybody else is saying. Yet all the while they think they're having the time of their lives, and you must sit there until midnight whether you want to or not.

Erasmus, *Colloquies*, 1523

Erasmus preferred French inns to German ones, and spoke with particular affection of the inns of Lyons, with their 'laughing, jolly sportive girls'. 'That's a spot,' he wrote, 'the companions of Ulysses couldn't have been torn away from. The Sirens are there. No one is treated better in his own home.' Smollett, travelling in France two and a half centuries later, took a very different view of French hospitality, and roundly cursed the whole tribe of French innkeepers.

Through the whole south of France, the inns are cold, damp, dark, dismal, and dirty; the landlords equally disobliging and rapacious; the servants awkward, sluttish, and slothful; and the postilions lazy, lounging, greedy, and impertinent. If you chide them for lingering, they will continue to delay you the longer: if you chastise them with sword, cane, cudgel, or horse-whip, they will either disappear entirely, and leave you without resource; or they will find means to take vengeance by overturning your carriage. The best method I know of travelling with any degree of comfort, is to allow yourself to become the dupe of imposition, and stimulate their endeavours by extraordinary gratifications.

Tobias Smollett, *Travels through France and Italy*, 1766

*Dr Johnson and Boswell, when they toured the High-
lands together, in 1773, spent a miserable night at an
inn at Glenelg. Here is how Dr Johnson describes it in
his* Journey to the Western Islands:

We were told that at Glenelg, on the sea-side, we
should come to a house of lime and slate and glass.
This image of magnificence raised our expectation. At
last we came to our inn weary and peevish, and began
to inquire for meat and beds.

Of the provisions the negative catalogue was very
copious. There was no meat, no milk, no bread, no
eggs, no wine. We did not express much satisfaction.
Here however we were to stay. Whisky we might have,
and I believe at last they caught a fowl and killed it.
We had some bread, and with that we prepared ourselves to be contented.

We were now to examine our lodging. Out of one
of the beds, on which we were to repose, started up, at
our entrance, a man black as a Cyclops from the forge.
Sleep, however, was necessary. Our Highlanders had at
last found some hay, with which the inn could not
supply them. I directed them to bring a bundle into
the room, and slept upon it in my riding coat. Mr
Boswell being more delicate, laid himself sheets with
hay over and under him, and lay in linen like a
gentleman.

Samuel Johnson, Journey to the Western
Islands, 1773

*And here is Boswell's account of the same dismal
hovel:*

We came on to the inn at Glenelg. There was no
provender for our horses; so they were sent to grass,
with a man to watch them. A maid shewed us up
stairs into a room damp and dirty, with bare walls,
a variety of bad smells, a coarse black greasy fir table,
and forms of the same kind; and out of a wretched bed
started a fellow from his sleep, like Edgar in King
Lear, 'Poor Tom's a cold.'

Our bad accommodation made me uneasy, and almost fretful. Dr Johnson was calm. I said, he was so from vanity. – *Johnson.* 'No, sir, it is from philosophy.' – It pleased me to see that the *Rambler* could practise so well his own lessons.

I sent for fresh hay, with which we made beds for ourselves, each in a room equally miserable. Like Wolfe, we had a '*choice of difficulties.*' Dr Johnson made things easier by comparison. At M'Queen's, last night, he observed, that few were so well lodged in a ship. To-night he said, we were better than if we had been upon the hill. He lay down buttoned up in his great coat. I had my sheets spread on the hay, and my clothes and great coat laid over me, by way of blankets.

> James Boswell, *Journal of a Tour to the*
> *Hebrides*, 1773

A twentieth-century traveller in the region, A. M. W. Stirling, found the inn at Glenelg even less appealing in 1913 than it had been in 1773.

Johnson has celebrated the horrors of the inn at Glenelg, at which we at last arrived; but since his time it has grown worse. There was nothing at all to eat, beds there were none, there was not even a chair! There was indeed a room which they offered *either* to *us or our horses!*

> A. M. W. Stirling, *Macdonald of the Isles*, 1913

Sometimes it is the food which is the ultimate turn-off. S. J. Perelman describes the restaurant of the Western and Occidental Hotel in the port of George-town on the island of Penang.

I doubt if anyone short of Dante could describe the cookery at the Western and Occidental Hotel; I have heard it defended on the ground that it is no worse than the fare in any British colonial hotel, which is like saying that measles is no worse than virus pneumonia. The meal usually led off with an eerie gumbo identified as pumpkin soup, puce in color and

dysenteric in effect. This was followed by a crisp
morsel of the fish called *selangor* for want of a more
scathing term, reminiscent in texture of a Daniel Green
comfy slipper fried in deep fat. The roast was a pale,
resilient scintilla of mutton that turned the tines of
the fork, garnished with a spoonful of greenish boiled
string and a dab of penicillin posing as a potato. For
dessert there was *gula Malacca*, a glutinous blob of
sago swimming in skimmed milk and caramel syrup,
so indescribably saccharine that it produced a singing
in the ears and screams of anguish from the bridge-
work. As the diner stiffened slowly in his chair, his
features settling into the ghastly smile known as the
risus sardonicus, the waiter administered the *coup de
grâce*, a savory contrived of a moldy sardine spread-
eagled on a bit of blackened toast. The exact nature
of the thimbleful of rusty brown fluid that concluded
the repast was uncertain. The only other time I saw it,
awash in the scuppers of the *President Monroe*, the
sailors called it bilge.

S. J. Perelman, *Westward Ha!*, 1959

*There is an old saw about a man travelling in Ireland
who stopped at a village where there were only two
hotels, Murphy's and Finn's. He asked a policeman
which was the better. The policeman answered: 'Well,
it's somewhat hard for me to say, seeing they are both
good friends of mine. But I can tell you, Sir, that
whichever hotel you choose, you will be sure to wish
that you had chosen the other.' Eric Newby was faced
with a similarly unenviable choice on a visit to Bijnor
in Northern India.*

It was now three-thirty and we had breakfasted thinly.
So far as we could discover there were only two places
in which it was even remotely possible to eat, and both
on inspection proved to be so loathsome that it seemed
tantamount to suicide to patronise either, but there is
something about the air of Asia which engenders an
emptiness that is unlike anything one experiences in

the West. Without food one's legs begin to feel like jelly. At this moment we were all three suffering from these symptoms and, in spite of the fact that our impulse was to patronise neither restaurant, we entered the Evergreen Hotel.

Evergreen and Hotel in name only, to us it was the quintessence of everything that Bijnor had come to signify. The floor was littered with unwanted food. On the greasy tables the contents of the capless ketchup bottles had long since coagulated, and the air was filled with the restless drone of bluebottles going about their business. Appalled, we sought shelter in an inner, darker room where two local inhabitants, friendly professional men, were lingering over the remains of their meal. It was difficult to imagine the contingency that had driven them to eat in such a place when, as they later admitted, they had homes of their own to go to in the city. This inner room was entirely bare of ornament, apart from two tiers of stone shelves. The only illumination came from a fanlight in the roof. It was more like a mortuary than a place to eat. One of the two diners, both of whom were lawyers, offered us his card. 'This is a very dirty restaurant,' he remarked cheerfully. 'It is better to eat cooked foods.'

We gave our order to a small, intelligent-looking boy who answered to the name of Vishnu. After a short interval he reappeared with some chapatis which he kept clamped to a plate by a grimy thumb. 'If you are Vishnu you should be four-handed. You are contaminating the food with your dirty fingers,' the lawyer who had given us his card shouted – and to us, 'It is useless to remonstrate with such people, they have no idea of hygiene.'

Vishnu grinned. 'The hands of Vishnu are already filled,' he answered pertly, but when he arrived with the tea he removed his fingers from the inside of the teacups before putting them down on the table. The lawyer had a good laugh at this. 'That boy,' he said, 'is a very witty boy. He is saying that although Vishnu has four hands they are filled. This is true. Vishnu has shell in one hand, discus in second hand, club in third hand and lotus in fourth hand. He is clever boy; but he has dirty fingers.'

Of all the awful meals that I have ever been called upon to consume, this was one of the worst. Vile, greasy gobbets of unidentifiable meat floated in a loathsome sauce and there were little pots of pale, watery lentil. G.'s vegetable curry was an affront to the senses. Everything had the dankness of left-overs. Our gorges rose and we rejected the meat and the vegetables; but because we were starving and in spite of the thought of Vishnu's fingers, we toyed with the chapatis which were like rubber tobacco pouches and drank luke-warm tea. Even so we knew that we were running into danger. Perhaps Vishnu was not really Vishnu at all, but an embodiment of Kali, The Destroyer.

Outside in the road again we were confronted by a sign over a doctor's establishment. 'Consult in all kinds diseases,' it read. '1. Phthisis. 2. Catarrh. 3. Fever. 4. Sterility. 5. Medical Certificates. 6. Constipation. 7. All kinds weaknesses. 8. Birth Control.'

'If we are staying here we are having all these,' G. said gloomily.

Eric Newby, *Slowly Down the Ganges*, 1966

Large anonymous hotels can be depressing at any season, but become intolerable when you are the only guest. James Cameron recalls the horrors of a beach hotel in Albania.

About five miles outside Durres stood the new beach hotel called the Adriatika. It was one of several hotels that faced the sea in various conditions of half-completion. They had all clearly been erected by the Russians for their use as a resort, and when the rift came they had been abandoned. Only the Adriatika was operational, and of its three hundred rooms the only ones in occupation were ours.

It had been designed in what might be called the Soviet Black Sea taste – that is to say, the layout was of an elaboration and grandeur that could only be justified by its fulfilment in costly and sumptuous materials. It had, however, been run up in a hurry and on a shoestring; instead of fine timbers and rich marbles there was plasterboard and gritty cement; in the spacious hall the evergreen plants grew out of oil drums painted green. In my bedroom the divan was so placed that in order to go to bed one had to move the wardrobe, and to open the wardrobe it was necessary to move the bed. The overall effect was exasperating, and lowering.

The food was almost indescribably terrible. I am no gastronome at the best, moreover. I have, over the years, eaten in so many unpropitious circumstances and from so many truly awful kitchens that I have come to consider myself almost as much a connoisseur of bad food as other men are of good. But here in Durres was something that transcended anything I can remember. It is very hard to define its nature, other than to say that it was Balkan food taken to its final and desperate conclusion: pasta that had been cooked, or apparently so, many days before, then passed through some compressing process: vague and improbable cuts of antique meat subjected to brief and inadequate heat; hollow tomatoes filled with a kind of herbal sawdust. It puzzled me that there should be no fish at all, until the explanation dawned: there were no fishermen. There were no fishermen because there were no boats. With Italy only fifty miles away across the Adriatic, who would let a fisherman over the horizon, since he would most assuredly never come back?

One crushing disappointment crowned the week: here

was the first place in the whole world where I found
one totally undrinkable wine – which is not said
lightly, since I had always been of the impression that
I could drink almost anything.

James Cameron, *Point of Departure*, 1967

*We give the last word in this section to that most
observant of hotel-watchers, Charles Dickens. In his*
Uncommercial Traveller, *he portrays a series of truly
awful hotels. Here is one of them:*

Mr Grazinglands, of the Midland Counties, came to
London by railroad one morning last week, accom-
panied by the amiable and fascinating Mrs Grazinglands. Mr G. is a gentleman of a comfortable property,
and had a little business to transact at the Bank of
England, which required the concurrence and signature
of Mrs G. Their business disposed of, Mr and Mrs
Grazinglands viewed the Royal Exchange, and the
exterior of St Paul's Cathedral. The spirits of Mrs
Grazinglands then gradually beginning to flag, Mr
Grazinglands (who is the tenderest of husbands) remarked with sympathy, 'Arabella, my dear, I fear you
are faint.' Mrs Grazinglands replied, 'Alexander, I am
rather faint; but don't mind me, I shall be better presently.' Touched by the feminine meekness of this
answer, Mr Grazinglands looked in at a pastry-cook's
window, hesitating as to the expediency of lunching
at that establishment . . . He might have entered, but
for the timely remembrance coming upon him that
Jairing's was but round the corner.

Now, Jairing's being an hotel for families and gentlemen, in high repute among the midland counties, Mr
Grazinglands plucked up a great spirit when he told
Mrs Grazinglands she should have a chop there. That
lady likewise felt that she was going to see Life.
Arriving on that gay and festive scene, they found the
second waiter, in a flabby undress, cleaning the
windows of the empty coffee-room; and the first waiter,
denuded of his white tie, making up his cruets behind

the Post-Office Directory. The latter (who took them in hand) was greatly put out by their patronage, and showed his mind to be troubled by a sense of the pressing necessity of instantly smuggling Mrs Grazinglands into the obscurest corner of the building. This slighted lady (who is the pride of her division of the county) was immediately conveyed, by several dark passages, and up and down several steps, into a penitential apartment at the back of the house, where five invalided old plate-warmers leaned up against one another under a discarded old melancholy sideboard, and where the wintry leaves of all the dining-tables in the house lay thick. Also, a sofa, of incomprehensible form regarded from any sofane point of view, murmured 'Bed'; while an air of mingled fluffiness and heeltaps, added, 'Second Waiter's'. Secreted in this dismal hold, objects of a mysterious distrust and suspicion, Mr Grazinglands and his charming partner waited twenty minutes for the smoke (for it never came to a fire), twenty-five minutes for the sherry, half an hour for the table-cloth, forty minutes for the knives and forks, three-quarters of an hour for the chops, and an hour for the potatoes. On settling the little bill – which was not much more than the day's pay of a Lieutenant in the navy – Mr Grazinglands took heart to remonstrate against the general quality and cost of his reception. To whom the waiter replied, substantially, that Jairing's made it a merit to have accepted him on any terms: 'for,' added the waiter (unmistakably coughing at Mrs Grazinglands, the pride of her division of the county), 'when indiwiduals is not staying in the 'Ouse, their favours is not as a rule looked upon as making it worth Mr Jairing's while; nor is it, indeed, a style of business Mr Jairing wishes'. Finally, Mr and Mrs Grazinglands passed out of Jairing's hotel for Families and Gentlemen, in a state of the greatest depression, scorned by the bar; and did not recover their self-respect for several days.

Charles Dickens, *The Uncommercial Traveller*, 1860

A Host of Hosts

In the four parts of the earth are many that are able to write learned books, many that are able to lead armies, and many also that are able to govern kingdoms and empires; but few there be that can keep a hotel.

attributed to Omar Khayyám

Ritz's widow tells what it takes to be the manager of a great hotel.

The hotel is a home, a workshop, a place of amusement, a station between journeys, a temple of the Arts (sometimes!), a parade-ground, a meeting-place; it is a part of the big world, and it is also a world unto itself. Over this small world presides the manager, who must be something more than a frock-coated major-domo, financier, dietitian, and policeman, but must upon occasion be lawyer and confessor – with their supreme discretion.

Marie Louise Ritz, *César Ritz*, 1938

Here is another, rather less flattering, view of the managerial role:

In a hotel like the Splendide, it must be assumed, for the purposes of good management, that every guest is a distinguished and elegant person who, of course, has a great deal of money. The prices are high and must be high; the cost of provisions is probably the smallest item. The charges are for marble columns, uniforms, thick carpets, fine linen, thin glasses, many servants, and a good orchestra. And the management of such a hotel is a difficult, delicate business. It produces in most cases a type of man whose face is like a towel on which everyone has wiped both hands, a smooth,

smiling, bowing man, in ever freshly pressed clothes,
a flower in his lapel, précieux and well fed.

Ludwig Bemelmans, *Hotel Bemelmans*, 1946

*One of the trickier problems to face the hotelier is how
– diplomatically! – to attract the right crowd and repel
the wrong.*

Among the brilliant throng that frequented the Savoy
were some – not so brilliant. Ritz had induced the best
society to dine there. But if these others, chiefly ladies
of doubtful reputation and uncertain revenue, were
allowed to frequent the place too much, what then?
Yet how avoid offending some of these 'ladies' who
brought along their princely partners of the moment?
They were too ornamental, too influential, to turn
away. But the others! Decidedly, something must be
done!

Ritz ordained that evening dress was *de rigueur* in
the dining-rooms. Ladies with hats or ladies unac-
companied by gentlemen could not be admitted
(Another Ritz precedent that has since been always
followed.) The effect was magical.

'You can lay down the law now,' said Liane de
Pougy, laughing airily. 'For you have reached the
height of your career in your profession – as I have
in mine!'

'Alas,' said Ritz, 'I am afraid with far less pleasure
and far more trouble than you have experienced,
mademoiselle!'

Marie Louise Ritz, *César Ritz*, 1938

In the hierarchy of the grand hotel, the maître d'hôtel
*stands one rung down from the Manager. Ludwig
Bemelmans, in his immortal* Hotel Bemelmans, *offers
portraits of several princes of the species. Here is
Monsieur Victor of the Splendide:*

Victor's salary from the hotel is not large, only $350
a month, plus his food, a dressing room, linen, and a
valet; but his income in a good year is about $40,000.

Society contributes little of that, and they treat him badly, but no matter when they arrive and in what mood or unexpected numbers, he will bow deeply, address them loudly by name, so that all the other waiting guests may be properly impressed, and seat them immediately. He is very careful not to address one of their women by her last year's name. Their complaints are immediately attended to, and when they leave they are again bowed out with a compliment that would cost other people at least twenty dollars. All that because, without them, the restaurant is through, and would be closed in a short while.

But other guests, too, may receive good tables, after they have stuck a little folded bill into Monsieur Victor's hand. When he is not certain from experience of the size of the bill, he always hears an imaginary telephone bell ringing and rushes into his office. Attached to the wall at the level of his hand is a mirror; in it Victor can see whether there is five or ten dollars printed on the corner of the bill, and, around Christmas time, whether it is twenty, fifty, or a hundred. During the five hasty steps that take him back to the door, he has performed a lightning-quick calculation, an exercise in the nice adjustment of many factors: the available table, the time of the day, the day of the week, and the amount of the bank note. The assistant hears a softly pronounced table number, and the guests are led to a table. If they are delighted or make faces, the little mirror in the office knows why.

Ludwig Bemelmans, *Hotel Bemelmans*, 1946

Small hotels, run by resident owners, can afford to take a cavalier line with undesirables. John Fothergill, innkeeper-extraordinary of the Spreadeagle at Thame, near Oxford, in the 1920s, lays down the tenets of his profession.

Here I've determined not only to have proper and properly cooked food but to have only either intelligent, beautiful or well-bred people to eat it. Although barely paying our way, we've declined dozens of applications for rooms simply because we don't know the people, or the writing or the address don't please. To several of the commoner undergraduates I have said that I don't want them here with indiscriminate girls, and yet some people will argue with me that I am compelled by law to take them in or feed them! My answer is, 'Either I give them bread and cheese in a back room, or fill the place rapidly with men and prostitutes or the undesirable kind of undergraduate and let go the polite atmosphere that pervades the place and our polite staff too.' Few realize what I go through to get and keep for it the atmosphere this place now has. After all, Innkeeping is the only profession where one's business is also one's home. If it be thought eccentric or arrogant to encourage only certain kinds of people to share your roof and floor, is this not, in fact, always done? The beery Innkeeper has beery friends and discourages the others and so on, and the man who has no particular character or leanings makes a characterless business of it.

John Fothergill, *An Innkeeper's Diary*, 1931

At times, he carried his prejudices to bizarre lengths.

Last Sunday we had thirty-nine folks to tea and I
noticed that they were almost all ill-shaped, ugly or ill-
dressed. I came into the office and complained at having
to work for such people at 1s. 6d. a head. Charles
Neilson said, 'That's easy – put up a notice, "Buy
our masks at 1s. each, or pay 6d. extra."' So I went
in and told Phyllis to charge 6d. face-money each for
the worst cases. Thus for the first time in history seven
people without knowing it have left an inn having
paid 6d. each for not being beautiful. And surely this
was a more praiseworthy action than the usual one of
charging people extra because they *are* beautiful, well
bred and dressed?

John Fothergill, Ibid.

*The landlady, traditionally, has been a figure of
ridicule or contempt or else has been treated as a
rapacious virago, as in this passage from* Tom Jones.

The landlady refused to suffer any removals till after
the payment of the reckoning. The landlady was
absolute governess in these regions; it was therefore
necessary to comply with her rules; so the bill was
presently writ out, which amounted to a much larger
sum than might have been expected, from the enter-
tainment which Jones had met with. But here we are
obliged to disclose some maxims, which publicans hold
to be the grand mysteries of their trade. The first
is, if they have anything good in their house (which
indeed very seldom happens) to produce it only to
persons who travel with great equipages. Secondly to
charge the same for the very worst provisions, as if
they were the best. And, lastly, if any of their guests
call but for little, to make them pay a double price
for everything they have; so that the amount by the
head may be much the same.

Henry Fielding, *Tom Jones,* 1749

Arnold Bennett tells of a landlady with a redeeming sense of humour:

Montlucon, July – I was looking for rooms in a hotel near the railway. As the landlady and I went along a corridor upstairs, I said I hoped the noise of trains could not be heard in the bedrooms. 'One hears nothing,' she answered positively. She opened the door of a room, and a tremendous engine-shriek met us, seeming to drive us both back from the threshold. She shut the door, and tried another one, and we were met instantly by another tremendous engine-shriek. She burst out laughing. I laughed too. If she had not proved her sense of humour I might have walked straight out of the hotel. But her sense of humour kept a customer with a sense of humour. I got quiet rooms at the back.

Arnold Bennett, *Journals*, 1929

Blackpool landladies have been pilloried more than any other of their breed. In the high season, they would be shameless in packing visitors in – as illustrated in this sketch by a humorous writer from Rochdale:

Plenty of room, gentlemen. I have often had thirty people sleeping in the house, and never more than seven in a bed. We shall make you comfortable somewhere. The parlour table holds five – three long way and two across – and if that should be full we can make you quite snug on the floor. Last summer we were rather pushed, so I fitted a board over the scullery sink for two youngsters to sleep on, and swung a hammock in the cellar steps with a breadth of carpet and the clothes line . . . It was the coolest place in the house, so I charged sixpence extra for it.

Trafford Clegg, *Rochdale Observer*, 1890

But of course not all Blackpool landladies deserved execration. Many became close friends with their guests who returned year after year. Here is a tribute from one such grateful and constant visitor:

We used to do our own buying in when we got there and we had a shelf in a cupboard where we left them and each day we would go and buy our own meat or fish for the day and Mrs Cavanagh did all the cooking and everything was lovely. Mr Cavanagh was in the background doing all the washing up etc. We went each year and she had something altered in the house each time. We still went after we were married and it cost us 28s. per week for a double bed and all the cooking ... We went thirteen years running three times a year, it was like home from home. I remember one very wet day and Mrs Cavanagh said you all have no need to go out at all. After dinner was cleared she brought out the cards, and we were all having such a good time when who should come in but the landlady, a white bucket filled with ice cream and wafers to go with it, she had been to Pablo's round the corner and had it filled. She was a grand person and there was always tears as we had to leave. My husband was the only chap she would give a pint pot of tea to, all the others had to have cups.

Mrs Eleanor Schofield quoted in *The Blackpool Landlady* by John K. Walton, 1978

They Also Serve

Cooks, though below stairs, can make or mar a hotel's reputation. Alice of Alice's Restaurant fame had a disastrous if short-lived spell in charge of the kitchens at the Orpheus Ascending Inn in the Berkshire Hills of Massachusetts.

Rebecca, our chef, took ill, and remembering that Alice Brock, who had formerly owned Alice's Restaurant, was at liberty, I called her. Alice is a tall, sensual woman with a strong personality. In our first confrontation I said (diplomatically, I thought), 'Now, Alice, this is a French restaurant and in your place you cooked Russian and Middle Eastern food. Do you think you can manage it?'

'I can cook anything,' she replied.

'Yes, but can you cook it French?' I pressed.

'Let me see your menu,' she asked.

We studied it together.

'No problem,' she scoffed. 'But, Steve, I have to have carte blanche in the choice of dishes, do my own ordering and work with my own assistant. Okay?'

'It will have the French touch though, Alice?' I asked nervously.

'Now, if you don't have faith in me . . .' She flailed her arms, looking like Phaedra hailing an Athenian ship.

Alice was a celebrity due to the Arlo Guthrie film *Alice's Restaurant*, and I felt her notoriety would be good publicity for Orpheus. 'I have faith,' I declared. And then, as she hadn't seemed to hear me, I repeated, 'I said I have faith in you, Alice.'

'And I need my own waiter, too,' she added.

I had large posters printed proclaiming, 'Alice Is

Cooking At Orpheus Ascending!' Since Alice is an illustrator as well as a cook, I suggested she design the posters herself so that we could sell them in the gallery. (I suspect we took in more cash from the sale of the posters than we did from the sale of the food.)

Two days before she was to begin her 'engagement' the cartons started arriving. Cases of buckwheat, groats and orzo. We had our second confrontation.

'Alice,' I screamed, 'you said you would keep to a French menu!'

'And you said you had faith!' she screamed back.

'I never heard of a French dish with buckwheat, groats or orzo,' I countered.

She handed me a copy of a menu she had printed. It was in French, though I had not heard of one dish.

'Faith,' she repeated, and opening one of the refrigerators, she took out a chilled bottle of red wine. I gasped. The refrigerator was loaded with red wine. 'Now, am I the chef or you?' she demanded, hugging the gallon bottle to her ample breast.

It was going to be impossible for me to take over the kitchen and still carry on with everything I had to do. Also, it had already been advertised that Alice was cooking for Orpheus.

'Okay, Alice,' I agreed, 'you're the chef, but I'm the boss. No chilled red wine. I abhor chilled red wine.'

'I believe in the importance of wine in cooking – some in the stew, some in the cook.' She laughed as she poured herself a glass.

The first night of her reign, plates filled with rice and pasta and beans sallied forth from the kitchen. I stormed through the swinging door and faced her. 'You are serving rice *and* pasta *and* beans!' I shouted.

'What's wrong with that?' she demanded.

'To begin with, it's not French – and to end with, it's too heavy,' I replied angrily.

'They don't have to eat all three,' she said quite calmly, stirring a steaming pot, 'but let them be there.'

The next morning the kitchen was filled with containers of leftovers, which she was giving to all the employees to take home. When I complained, she said, 'Leftovers toughen,' which she stated as if it were an axiom. If that was the truth, it was a sorry one for me, since I was paying the bills. It is impossible to resent Alice though, for she is like the 'mother-of-us-all'. She is compulsive and wants to feed everyone in sight, believing no one should leave a table unless stuffed. I could see that our relationship had to be of short duration or I would go broke. Besides I didn't want to turn Orpheus into a Middle Eastern restaurant no matter how appropriate the name. So as soon as Rebecca mended, Alice and I came to a parting of the ways. (If the reader wants a poster of Alice cooking or a box of orzo, let them just write to me, I have a whole supply.)

Anne Edwards and Steven Citron,
The Inn and Us, 1976

One of the classics of 'kitchen' literature is George Orwell's Down and Out in Paris and London. *Here, Orwell describes his work as a washer-up and waiter on waiters in the Hotel X, Paris.*

My bad day was when I washed up for the dining-room. I had not to wash the plates, which were done in the kitchen, but only the other crockery, silver, knives and glasses; yet, even so, it meant thirteen hours' work, and I used between thirty and forty dish-cloths during the day. The antiquated methods used in France double the work of washing up. Plate-racks are unheard of, and there are no soap-flakes, only the treacly soft soap, which refuses to lather in the hard Paris water. I worked in a dirty, crowded little den, a pantry and scullery combined, which gave straight on the dining-room. Besides washing up, I had to fetch the waiters' food and serve them at table: most of them were intolerably insolent, and I had to use my fists more than once to get common civility.

It was amusing to look round the filthy little scullery and think that only a double door was between us and the dining-room. There sat the customers in all their splendour – spotless table-clothes, bowls of flowers, mirrors and gilt cornices and painted cherubim; and here, just a few feet away, we in our disgusting filth. For it really was disgusting filth. There was no time to sweep the floor till evening, and we slithered about in a compound of soapy water, lettuce-leaves, torn paper and trampled food. A dozen waiters with their coats off showing their sweaty armpits, sat at the table mixing salad and sticking their thumbs into the cream pots. The room had a dirty, mixed smell of food and sweat. Everywhere in the cupboards, behind the piles of crockery, were squalid stores of food that the waiters had stolen. There were only two sinks and no washing basin, and it was nothing unusual for a waiter to wash his face in the water in which clean crockery was rinsing. But the customers saw nothing of this. There were a coco-nut mat and a mirror outside the dining-room door, and the waiters used to preen themselves up and go in making the picture of cleanliness.

George Orwell, *Down and Out in Paris and London*, 1933

Arnold Bennett sketches a cloakroom attendant at the Savoy Hotel, London.

Tale of the head of the cloakroom; been there for ages; remembers people's faces, often without troubling as to their names. He took an overcoat from an old gentleman, and gave it back to him at the end without a word.

GUEST: How did you know that this is mine?
EMPLOYEE: I don't know, sir.
GUEST: Then why do you give it to me?
EMPLOYEE: Because you gave it to me, sir.

Arnold Bennett, *Journals*, 1924

Hotel staff in smart hotels are often accused of snootiness, especially the clerk in reception.

Christians who are always striving to humble and abase themselves – whose besetting sin is pride – should take a dose of hotel clerk. Whenever I feel that I need taking down a peg or two, and that I am getting too big for my clothes, I have a never-failing remedy. I merely step into a first-class hotel, and approach Mr Diamond Pin, and ask: 'Is Mr. Smith stopping here?' The great man, after four or five minutes, lifts his eyes, he speaks. I am crushed.

A. Emerson Belcher, *What I know about Commercial Travelling*, 1893

Here is another view of what it feels like to be at the receiving end of the disdainful brush-off, grand hotel style:

It is the boast of Barribault's Hotel, which caters principally to American millionaires and visiting maha-

rajahs, that it can make the wrong sort of client feel
more like a piece of cheese – and a cheap yellow piece
of cheese at that – than any other similar establishment in the world. The personnel of its staff are
selected primarily for their ability to curl the upper lip
and raise the eyebrows just that extra quarter of an
inch which makes all the difference.

Bill was a splendidly virile young man, and if you
had had a mad bull you wished dealt with, you could
have placed it in no better hands. But there are times
when this business of being large and muscular pays
no dividends, and in the super-aristocratic interior of
Barribault's you are better served by a slim elegance
and up-to-the-minute tailoring.

By nature diffident, and conscious that his clothes,
however admirably suited to some Bohemian revel at a
Chelsea studio, were out of place in this temple of the
best people, Bill had been reduced by his interview
with a polished plenipotentiary in the dining-room to
a state of almost soluble discomfort. It was all too
plain to him that the plenipotentiary did not like his
tie and was surprised and resentful that anyone in such
baggy trousers should be proposing to lunch on the
premises. He had tottered out feeling that his hands
and feet had been affected by some sort of elephantiasis
and that his outer appearance was that of a tramp
cyclist.

P. G. Wodehouse, *Full Moon*, 1947

*A switchboard operator is an altogether more modest
member of the hotel staff. Jonathan Raban writes of
one he met in a Cairo hotel.*

The switchboard operator sat in her booth in the hotel;
a patient lady with a heavy, pharaonic face. Her
apparatus was ancient and vastly complicated. Lights
flashed on and off, plugs were pushed in and yanked
out: the technical dexterity required to make one telephone call was immense. Given a number to dial, she

would smile sadly, take a deep breath, and bury herself in her machinery. The expression on her face during these operations was painful to watch. She looked like an airline pilot trying to land a jet in thick fog with two engines gone and the navigation system dead. Usually she failed: the call would stall, overshoot, or just break up somewhere in the wires. Occasionally she succeeded, and if one held the phone close to one's ear, one could hear faint, squawking, metallic sounds which sometimes resolved themselves into words. At best, it was like getting a bad line to the moon.

I had heard that Jan Morris was staying at the Mena House Hotel, out near the pyramids, and I hoped that we might meet up for a drink or a meal.

'Oh dear, that is a very difficult number for me. Very difficult. But I will try.'

She did, and failed. After twenty minutes of terrible exertion she said: 'I am sorry. It is no good. I shall never reach the Mena House.'

'How do you tell "difficult" numbers from "easy" ones?'

'I have experience,' she said wearily. She held my hand: after perhaps a dozen joint assaults on the Cairo telephone system we had developed the natural intimacy of people who have had shared sufferings.

'Please, my dear,' she said. 'You must understand: Cairo is all out of connections.'

Jonathan Raban, Arabia Through the Looking Glass, 1979

Studs Terkel, the famous Chicago broadcaster, listens to a room clerk at a Manhattan hotel near Times Square.

I begin at eight in the morning. I have to have a smile on my face. Some mornings that's a little difficult. The first thing you run into is people checking out from the night before. You might get a slight lull and then people begin arriving. They're like little bees. You're concentrating on what you're doing. It's a little difficult to have that smile all the time. I have one particular girl who says to me, 'What? No smile this morning?' So I smile.

I doubt if a hotel clerk really commands a heck of a lot of respect. I've had people talk to me just like I was some sort of dog, that I was a ditch–digger, let's say. You figure a fellow who comes to work and he has to have a cleanly pressed suit and white shirt and a tie on – plus he's gotta have that big smile on his face – shouldn't be talked to in a manner that he's something so below somebody else.

It affects me. It gives you that feeling: Oh hell, what's the use? I've got to get out of this. Suddenly you look in the mirror and you find out you're not twenty-one any more. You're fifty-five. Many people have said to me, 'Why didn't you get out of it long ago?' I never really had enough money to get out. I was stuck, more or less.

My legs are quite tired. I'm on my feet the whole time. In doing these jobs I don't have much of a chance to sit down. You're moving back and forth and pivoting most of the time. You're not in a large area. You're turning and pivoting. Oft times through the day I take a walk in front of the desk.

The thing I don't like about it is you're trapped – in a small area eight hours a day. You're behind the desk. We had a grill on our desk and I asked them to take it away, because I felt like I was in jail.

The clerk in a hotel is rarely tipped. The bellboys, rather, get all the tips. A fellow that comes into the hotel to do a little cheating will always tip the bellboy heavily. The boy can't help him at all, in any way, shape, or form. It's the clerk who watches his mail, watches his messages, and watches who comes in and out to see him. It's really the clerk who covers for him. But he never seems to realize that.

The fellow relies on the bellboy to keep his mouth shut. The bellboys never keep their mouths shut. The first guy they tell is the clerk, when they come back –

if the clerk doesn't already know it. (Laughs.) Occasionally you will get people who seem to know their way around. They will throw the clerk a couple of bucks or a five-dollar bill now and then.

Everybody's in a rush: 'Will you *please* hurry up with my bill? I'm in a hurry, I gotta catch a plane.' It's a shame, because we could live in such a relaxed society . . .

I'm getting a little older. Can't take it the way I could twenty years ago. Sometimes you just sit and ponder the day. You get a lot of laughs. (Laughs.) A fellow walked in one morning, he wanted to know if I had seen his wife. He took a picture out of his pocket and held it up. He said, 'If you see her, tell her I was looking for her.' It was a picture of a nude woman. (Laughs.) You get a lot of laughs.

Studs Terkel, Working, 1974

Tipping – how much and to whom – is a perennial problem for travellers. Mark Twain contrasts European and American practices in the 1890s, with a strong preference for the former.

A word about the European hotel *portier*. He is a most admirable invention, a most valuable convenience. He always wears a conspicuous uniform; he can always be found when he is wanted, for he sticks closely to his post at the front door; he is as polite as a duke; he speaks from four to ten languages; he is your surest help and refuge in time of trouble or perplexity. The more requirements you can pile upon him, the better he likes it.

What is the secret of the portier's devotion? It is very simple: he gets *fees, and no salary.* His fee is pretty closely regulated, too. If you stay a week in the house, you give him five marks – a dollar and a quarter, or about eighteen cents a day. If you stay a month, you reduce this average somewhat. If you stay two or three months or longer, you cut it down half, or even more

[37]

than half. If you stay only one day, you give the portier a mark.

Fees are never paid until you leave the hotel, though it be a year. It is considered very bad policy to fee a servant while you are still to remain longer in the hotel, because if you gave him too little he might neglect you afterwards, and if you gave him too much he might neglect somebody else to attend to you. It is considered best to keep his expectations 'on a string' until your stay is concluded.

I do not know whether hotel servants in New York get any wages or not, but I do know that in some of the hotels there the feeing system in vogue is a heavy burden. The waiter expects a quarter at breakfast – and gets it. You have a different waiter at luncheon, and so he gets a quarter. Your waiter at dinner is another stranger – consequently he gets a quarter. The boy who carries your satchel to your room and lights your gas, fumbles around and hangs around significantly, and you fee him to get rid of him. Now you may ring for ice-water; and ten minutes later a lemonade; and ten minutes afterwards, for a cigar; and by and by for a newspaper – and what is the result? Why, a new boy has appeared every time, and fooled and fumbled around until you have paid him something. Suppose you boldly put your foot down, and say it is the hotel's business to pay its servants? – and suppose you stand your ground and stop feeing? You will have to ring your bell ten or fifteen times before you get a servant there; and when he goes to fill your order you will grow old and infirm before you see him again. You may struggle nobly for twenty-four hours, may be, if you are an adamantine sort of person, but in the meantime you will have been so wretchedly served, and so insolently, that you will haul down your colours, and go to impoverishing yourself with fees.

Mark Twain, A *Tramp Abroad*, 1898

Dumb Waiter

We finish this section with literature's most celebrated bootboy: Sam Weller, making his first appearance in The Pickwick Papers *in the yard of the White Hart:*

In the yard of the White Hart, a man was busily employed in brushing the dirt off a pair of boots. He was habited in a coarse-striped waistcoat, with black calico sleeves, and blue glass buttons; drab breeches and leggings. A bright red handkerchief was wound in a very loose and unstudied style round his neck, and an old white hat was carelessly thrown on one side of his head. There were two rows of boots before him, one cleaned and the other dirty, and at every addition he made to the clean row, he paused from his work, and contemplated its results with evident satisfaction.

A loud ringing of one of the bells, was followed by the appearance of a smart chambermaid in the upper sleeping gallery, who called over the balustrades –

'Sam!'

'Hallo,' replied the man with the white hat.

'Number twenty-two wants his boots.'

'Ask number twenty-two, whether he'll have 'em now, or wait till he gets 'em,' was the reply.

'Come, don't be a fool, Sam,' said the girl, coaxingly, 'the gentleman wants his boots directly.'

'Well, you *are* a nice young 'ooman for a musical party, you are,' said the boot-cleaner. 'Look at these here boots – eleven pair o' boots; and one shoe as b'longs to number six, with the wooden leg. The eleven boots is to be called at half-past eight and the shoe at nine. Who's number twenty-two, that's to put all the others out? No, no; reg'lar rotation, as Jack Ketch said, wen he tied the men up. Sorry to keep you a waitin', sir, but I'll attend to you directly.'

Saying which, the man in the white hat set to work upon a topboot with increased assiduity.

There was another loud ring; and the bustling old landlady of the White Hart made her appearance in the opposite gallery.

'Sam,' cried the landlady, 'where's that lazy, idle – why, Sam – oh, there you are; why don't you answer?'

'Wouldn't be gen-teel to answer, 'till you'd done talking,' replied Sam, gruffly.

'Here, clean them shoes for number seventeen directly, and take 'em to private sitting-room, number five, first floor.'

The landlady flung a pair of lady's shoes into the yard, and bustled away.

'Number 5,' said Sam, as he picked up the shoes, and taking a piece of chalk from his pocket, made a memorandum of their destination on the soles – 'Lady's shoes and private sittin'-room! I suppose *she* didn't come in the waggin.'

'She came in early this morning,' cried the girl, who was still leaning over the railing of the gallery, 'with a gentleman in a hackney coach, and it's him as wants his boots, and you'd better do 'em, that's all about it.'

'Vy didn't you say so before?' said Sam, with great indignation, singling out the boots in question from the heap before him. 'For all I know'd he vas one o' the regular three-pennies. Private room! and a lady too! If he's anything of a gen'lm'n, he's vorth a shillin' a day, let alone the arrands.'

Charles Dickens, *The Pickwick Papers*, 1837

[40]

Guests of Honour &
Dishonour

*The literature of hotels is as full of perfectly terrible
guests, misbehaving in a variety of outrageous ways as
it is of long-suffering victims of exploitation. But some
guests can be exceptionally sympathetic.*

This evening a man and two women turned up for
the night. Dinner came and they were the only people,
and after I had cooked and they had eaten it I went
into the dining-room. The man, seeing me coming,
turned round and called out across the deserted room,
'Well done!' I told him that this spontaneous ejacula-
tion, such as an actor wants and gets, was the best
acknowledgement I'd ever had for my efforts. The
supreme gratification for a cook would be to go in
when his food had been perfect throughout and to be
greeted with clapping from twelve tables in the room.
Has it ever been done? Never, I suppose, but what a
happy and unique cook to get it!

John Fothergill, *An Innkeeper's Diary*, 1931

*Here is another Fothergill story, showing a guest nobly
turning the other cheek:*

Two days ago an old lady met me in the hall and
asked if this was the principal Hotel in Ascot. 'Well,
it might be' was my welcoming reply. 'Can we have a
room with 2 beds for the night?' – 'Yes, delighted. I'll
get your bags taken up.' – 'But I'd like to see the room'
– 'Oh, you want to inspect my rooms do you? – Kate,
this lady wants to inspect our rooms.' Kate went out
to her, and I went inside the office but I shouted out

[41]

from inside, 'Don't show her the verminous room.'
They stayed, did this distinguished delightful couple –
Francis St George Caulfield – once keeper of all the
elephants in Malay and now caretaker of his own
eighty years. As they were going off I said, 'I hope you
weren't hurt by my irritable reception of you, but
"rooms inspection" is a bug-bear of mine.' – 'Not at
all,' said Mrs Caulfield. 'But what did you think then?'
– 'I said to my husband "that man is perfectly mad".'
And so this lady in her age has learnt humour and
wisdom and tolerance instead of bitterness, scorn and
fight.

John Fothergill, Ibid.

*Many guests never dream of complaining, but are not
necessarily unobservant or indifferent.*

'I'M A NICE GUEST'

You know me, I'm a nice guest, I never complain, no
matter what kind of service I get. I'll go into a hotel
and stand at the front desk for a long time while the
desk clerk busies himself with some books or figures
and never bothers to notice me. Sometimes someone
arrives after I do and gets taken care of right away,
but I don't say a word. If the clerk can't find my
reservation or the room isn't ready, I'm nice about it.
When the bellmen seem annoyed that I have checked
in, I try not to take it personally.

When I go to eat, I'm thoughtful of the other
person. If I get a grouchy waiter or waitress who is
annoyed because I want to study the menu a bit, I'm
polite as I can be. I don't believe that rudeness in
return is the answer. You might say I wasn't raised
that way. And it's seldom I ever send anything back to
the kitchen. I've found people are just about always
disagreeable to me when I do. Life is short! Too short
for indulging in these unpleasant little scrimmages.

I am often too intimidated by the head waiter to
complain when I order a steak medium and it is served

almost raw. I never kick. I never nag. I never criticize. I wouldn't dream of making a scene, as I've seen some people doing in public places. I think that's awful. I'm a nice guest and I always give a tip. I'll tell you what else I am: I'M THE GUEST WHO NEVER COMES BACK.

From an anonymous leaflet issued by the Bermuda Trade Development Board

Some fastidious guests may be as observant as hotel inspectors.

Meanwhile, Roland had paused in his unpacking, and was sitting on the bed and examining the room as though it interested him. Its deficiencies, its perfunctory slipshodness interested him. He happened to be interested in rooms, and he was a man of detail.

His mental comments followed immediately upon his visual perceptions.

'No wardrobe. Now – where the devil – ? Faded green paint – dirty paper – strings of pink roses between black and white lines. One hook off door. Carpet – h'm – I wonder what a vacuum cleaner would fetch out of it. Brass bed, one knob missing. Yellow chest of drawers, one handle missing.'

He got up.

'I bet the drawers stick, and that the paper inside them is last year's *Daily Mail*.'

He was right.

His observations ran on.

'Swing mirror plugged into place with a wad of paper. Blind torn. Japanese mats on floor need burning. Slop pail minus a handle. Marble top of wash-hand stand stained. Tooth glass smeary. Over washing-stand advertisement of Jeyes' Fluid. Over mantelpiece, tariff and advertisement of local tradesmen. Sheets need mending. Blankets – yes – just so!'

He resumed his unpacking and his meditations.

'How many of these places have I stayed in during the last month? A dozen – I suppose. And only one decently run place in the dozen. Slovenly holes, especially in these cathedral places. Here's a great opportunity under the noses of our inn-keepers, and all they seem to think of is the booze and the "bar"!'

He put out his boots.

'The cheek of them – too. Give you every sort of slovenliness and inattention, and bad food, and then charge you top prices. No supervision, no discipline, no conscience.'

His sponge-bag was extracted from a brightly polished cavalry mess tin, the two halves of which found receptacles for his sponge, washing gloves, nail-brush and tooth-brush. He glanced at the cracked sponge-basin belonging to the inn.

'No thanks! Obviously – no. Now – if that tow-headed female downstairs did her job properly instead of – . O, well, that's the curse of these places; a lot of soaking fools, and yellow-headed women. But what I never can understand is – why – if people take on a job – they can't do it properly. And yet – not three in ten can. Socialism! What rot!'

Warwick Deeping, *Sorrell and Son*, 1921

The profession of hotel inspector has had scant treat-ment in literature. Indeed, the 'Pension Grillparzer' – a complete short story contained within John Irving's zany and scintillating novel, The World According to Garp – *is, so far as I know, the first fictional treatment of a subject potentially rich in humour and drama. What follows is only the opening of the story; hilarious and poignant events are about to happen.*

My father worked for the Austrian Tourist Bureau. It was my mother's idea that our family travel with him when he went on the road as a Tourist Bureau spy. My mother and brother and I would accompany him on his secretive missions to uncover the discourtesy, the dust, the badly cooked food, the shortcuts taken by Austria's restaurants and hotels and pensions. We were instructed to create difficulties whenever we could, never to order exactly what was on the menu, to

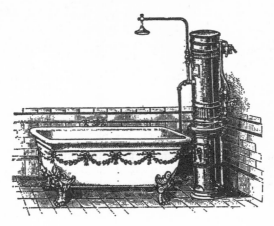

imitate a foreigner's odd requests – the hours we would like to have our baths, the need for aspirin and directions to the zoo. We were instructed to be civilised but troublesome; and when the visit was over, we reported to my father in the car.

My mother would say, 'The hairdresser is always closed in the morning. But they make suitable recommendations outside. I guess it's all right, provided they don't claim to have a hairdresser actually in the hotel.'

'Well, they do claim it,' my father would say. He'd note this in a giant pad.

I was always the driver. I said, 'The car is parked off the street, but someone put fourteen kilometers on the gauge between the time we handed it over to the doorman and picked it up at the hotel garage.'

'That is a matter to report directly to the management,' my father said, jotting it down.

'The toilet leaked,' I said.

'I couldn't open the door to the w.c.,' said my brother, Robo.

'Robo,' Mother said, 'you always have trouble with doors.'

'Was that supposed to be Class C?' I asked.

'I'm afraid not,' Father said. 'It is still listed as Class B.'

We drove for a short while in silence; our most serious judgment concerned changing a hotel's or a pension's rating. We did not suggest reclassification frivolously.

'I think this calls for a letter to the management,' Mother suggested.

'Not too nice a letter, but not a really rough one. Just state the facts.'

'Yes, I rather liked him,' Father said. He always made a point of getting to meet the managers.

'Don't forget the business of them driving our car,' I said. 'That's really unforgivable.'

'And the eggs were bad,' said Robo; he was not yet ten, and his judgments were not considered seriously.

John Irving, *The World According to Garp*, 1978

Halliday Sutherland reminds us of the universal truth – guests love to nurse a good grievance.

Back at the hotel I asked for my bill, as I would be leaving fairly early in the morning. I also told the head waitress that I would not be taking breakfast. There would be breakfast on the *Loch Fyne* at 8 a.m., and I never breakfast in hotels when it is possible to have breakfast on a steamer. Moreover, the hotel breakfast began at 8.30 a.m.

When she returned with the bill I saw that the not-to-be-eaten breakfast was charged at three shillings.

'But this is most unfair,' I said.

'It's the rule,' she replied, 'that bed and breakfast is eight shillings, and there's no reduction if you don't have breakfast.'

'I am not blaming you,' I continued quietly, 'but I would like you to realise how unfair it is. You are not only getting my three shillings but you are also getting the value of the breakfast, let us say one and six, which I shall not eat.'

'It's the rule,' she, woman like, persisted.

'I know it's the rule, but I would like you personally to realise that it is a most unfair rule not only to myself but to all other guests who may be sailing on the *Loch Fyne*.'

'The Boots can get up at seven and give you tea and boiled eggs.'

'No Boots shall rise at seven on account of me, and no Boots, not even the Boots at the Savoy Hotel, shall be allowed to prepare my breakfast. That is the privilege of a *chef*.' Then I paid the bill and knew that I had a genuine grievance on which I could feast my mind in moments of depression.

Halliday Sutherland, *Hebridean Journey*, 1939

For some guests, nothing is ever right or good enough.

'Madam,' said the landlady, 'I can get any kind of mutton in an instant from the butcher's.'

'Do you think then,' answered the waiting-gentle-woman, 'that I have the stomach of a horse to eat mutton at this time of night? Sure you people that keep inns imagine your betters are like yourselves. Indeed I expected to get nothing at this wretched place. I wonder my lady would stop at it. I suppose none but tradesmen and grasiers ever call here.' The landlady fired at this indignity offered to her house; however she suppressed her temper, and contented herself with saying, 'Very good quality frequent it, she thanked heaven!' 'Don't tell me,' cries the other, 'of quality! I believe I know more of people of quality than such as you. – But, prithee, without troubling me with any of your impertinence, do tell me what I can have for supper; for tho' I cannot eat horse-flesh, I am really hungry.' 'Why truly, madam,' answered the landlady, 'you could not have taken me again at such a disadvantage: for I must confess, I have nothing in the house, unless a cold piece of beef, which indeed a gentleman's footman, and the post-boy, have almost cleared to the bone.' 'Woman,' said Mrs Abigail (so for shortness we will call her) 'I intreat you not to make me sick. If I had fasted a month, I could not eat what had been touched by the fingers of such fellows: is there nothing neat or decent to be had in this horrid place?' 'What think you of some eggs and bacon, madam,' said the landlady. 'Are your eggs new laid? are you certain they were laid to-day? and let me have the bacon cut very nice and thin; for I can't endure anything that's gross. – Prithee try if you can do a little tolerably for once, and don't think you have a farmer's wife, or some of those creatures in the house.' – The landlady begun then to handle her knife; but the other stopt her, saying, 'Good woman, I must insist upon your first washing your hands; for I am extremely nice, and have been always used from my cradle to have everything in the most elegant manner.'

Henry Fielding, *Tom Jones*, 1749

When it comes to a row, innkeeper and guest may be evenly matched.

Three girls descended from a Lancia and went past me upstairs to the lavatory. I called out to the hindermost, 'Are you wanting lunch?' No answer. So I waited for them. They were inferior females got up to look grand. 'Did you leave anything upstairs for the housemaid?' and the front one began fumbling in her bag. I said, '*I* would have done so if I had rushed into *your* house without even asking your leave or saying "thank-you".' – 'But *is* it your house?' – 'Of course it is. I am licensed to sell beer here, and not to give water-closet accommodation to passers-by.' – 'They don't say anything, anyhow, at the Ritz and Berkeley.' – 'But those hotels are quite different and you would go unnoticed there.' – 'Yes, and they give you good manners.' – 'In return for bad,' I replied, and they got off.

John Fothergill, *An Innkeeper's Diary*, 1931

Unwelcome visitors may arrive in many guises. One of the less auspicious guests in fiction is the mysterious sea captain who takes the stage in the opening pages of Treasure Island.

I remember him as if it were yesterday, as he came plodding to the inn door, his sea-chest following behind him in a hand-barrow; a tall, strong, heavy, nut-brown man; his tarry pigtail falling over the shoulders of his soiled blue coat; his hands ragged and scarred, with black, broken nails; and the sabre cut across one cheek, a dirty, livid white. I remember him looking round the cove and whistling to himself as he did so, and then breaking out in that old sea-song that he sang so often afterwards:

> 'Fifteen men on the dead man's chest —
> Yo-ho-ho, and a bottle of rum!'

in the high old tottering voice that seemed to have been tuned and broken at the capstan bars. Then he rapped on the door with a bit of stick like a handspike that he carried, and when my father appeared, called roughly for a glass of rum. This, when it was brought to him, he drank slowly, like a connoisseur, lingering on the taste, and still looking about him at the cliffs and up at our signboard.

'This is a handy cove,' says he, at length; 'and a pleasant sittyated grog-shop. Much company, mate?'

My father told him no, very little company, the more was the pity.

'Well, then,' said he, 'this is the berth for me. Here you, matey,' he cried to the man who trundled the barrow; 'bring up alongside and help up my chest. I'll stay here a bit,' he continued. 'I'm a plain man; rum and bacon and eggs is what I want, and that head up there for to watch ships off. What you mought call me? You mought call me captain. Oh, I see what you're at — there'; and he threw down three or four gold pieces on the threshold. 'You can tell me when I've worked through that,' says he, looking as fierce as a commander.

He was a very silent man by custom. All day he hung round the cove, or upon the cliffs, with a brass telescope; all evening he sat in a corner of the parlour

next the fire, and drank rum and water very strong.
Mostly he would not speak when spoken to; only look
up sudden and fierce, and blow through his nose like
a fog-horn; and we and the people who came about our
house soon learned to let him be.

There were nights when he took a deal more rum
and water than his head would carry; and then he
would sometimes sit and sing his wicked, old, wild sea-
songs, minding nobody; but sometimes he would call
for glasses round, and force all the trembling company
to listen to his stories or bear a chorus to his singing.
Often I have heard the house shaking with 'Yo-ho-ho,
and a bottle of rum'; all the neighbours joining in for
dear life, with the fear of death upon them, and each
singing louder than the other, to avoid remark. For
in these fits he was the most overriding companion
ever known; he would slap his hand on the table for
silence all round; he would fly up in a passion of anger
at a question, or sometimes because none was put, and
so he judged the company was not following his story.
Nor would he allow anyone to leave the inn till he had
drunk himself sleepy and reeled off to bed.

Robert Louis Stevenson, *Treasure Island*, 1883

*In former times, innkeepers would often take the law
into their own hands in dealing with guests who
offended – especially those who failed to pay their bills.
In 1877, Potter Palmer of the Palmer House in Chicago
achieved notoriety when he and his staff stripped
several guests of their coats, cut off their trousers at
the knee and forced them to stand in the lobby with a
placard 'Hotel Deadbeat'. One, according to the Hotel
Mail, was forced to stand in front of the hotel thus
attired and labelled, after having been kept in his room
all day without food. But guests, too, could be quick to
take their revenge on landlords who offended. In this
respect, Benvenuto Cellini must have been in a class
of his own. Here he describes his revenge on an*

offending landlord in the course of a journey from Venice to Florence in 1535.

We lay one night at a place on this side of Chioggia. Here the host insisted upon being paid before we went to bed, according to his mode of reckoning, and when I observed that it was the custom everywhere else to pay in the morning, he answered: 'I want to be paid in the evening, and according to my own reckoning.' I retorted that men who wanted everything their own way ought to make a world after their own fashion, since things were managed differently in this world. Our host told me not to go on bothering his brains because he was determined to do as he had said. Tribolo stood trembling with fright and nudged me to keep quiet, lest things should be worse for us, so we paid him according to his way and went to bed.

We had, I must admit, the most capital beds, entirely new and very clean. For all this I could not sleep at all because I kept thinking how I could revenge myself. At one time it came into my head to set fire to his house; at another to cut the throats of four fine horses which he had in the stable. I saw clearly that it would be easy enough for me to do this but I could not see how it was easy to secure myself and my companion. At last I resolved to put my things and my comrade's on board the boat and so I did. When the horses had been harnessed to the tow-rope I told them not to start the boat until I returned for I had left a pair of slippers in my bedroom. Accordingly I went back to the inn and called the innkeeper who replied that he had nothing to do with us and we could go to blazes (*al bordello*). There was a ragged stable-boy about, half asleep, who cried out to me, 'The master would not move to please the Pope because he has got a wench in bed with him whom he has much coveted.' Then he asked me for a tip and I gave him a few Venetian coppers and told him to make the boatman wait until I had found my slippers and returned. I went upstairs, took out a small knife that cut like a razor, and cut the four beds that I found there into ribbons. I had the satisfaction of knowing that I had done a damage of more than fifty crowns. Then I ran down to the boat with some pieces of the bed-covers in my pouch and told the boatman to start at once. We had not gone far before my crony Tribolo said that he had left behind some small straps belonging to his travelling-bag and that he must be allowed to go back for them. I answered that he need not worry about two small straps since I could make him as many big ones as he liked (*coreggine* means fart as well as strap). He told me I was always joking but that he must really go back for his straps. Then he began ordering the man with the tow-rope to stop while I kept ordering him to go on. Meanwhile I informed my friend what kind of trick I had played on the innkeeper and showed him pieces of the bed-covers and other things. This threw him into such a trembling fright that he roared out to the tow-rope man: 'On with you, on with you, as quick as you can!' and never thought himself quite safe until we were within the gates of Florence.

Benvenuto Cellini, *Memoirs*, 1535

Russell Harty tells of a slightly less lethal revenge perpetrated by a film crew on an innocent waitress in a Blackpool boarding-house.

I was staying in Blackpool with a film crew, a bunch of sophisticated bruisers who would travel nowhere without their *Good Food Guide*. We were making, or hoping to make, a film in Blackpool. It was a last-minute decision and all the hotels with stars were filled with relaxed members of the Labour Party Conference. We found rooms in a boarding house. Not a hotel. The difference became all too dangerously clear. Lunch, with use of individual cruet, was being served.

The boarding house was unlicensed. Patience was at a low ebb. There was one girl serving. She had rules to obey. Somebody like Mrs Hesmondhaigh was not going to have any hanky-panky in her place. The serving girl brought in individual plates of nourishing roast and two veg. Hairy technicians began to tap the spotless table cloths and examine their used finger-nails. We were in the middle of the dining area, not room, and the maid had to do the outside tables, by order, before she started on us.

When she arrived with our plates, she made no apology for the intolerable delay, and she wiped the bottom of the plate before she laid it neatly, meat to the north, veg to the east and west, mash to the south, in front of each customer. One brave lad spoke up and asked for a jug of iced water. The girl looked perplexed and then said she would go and ask. We restrained our mirth.

She came back after a time and said that they didn't do jugs of iced water.

Why not?

She didn't know, but she would go and ask. She came back and said that the landlady had told her to tell us that this was a boarding house and not a hotel. You only got jugs of water in a hotel. In a boarding house, it was glasses. Thereupon, the Aswan High Dam of impatience cracked down the middle, and each thirsty member of the crew asked for a glass of water. The reddening maid began to suspect a dirty plot. The water went down in a gulp, and just as she had

started on her rounds with the jam sponge, there were
constant calls for more water. It was a truly frightening
experience. This thirsty pack was bent upon revenge
and intended, thereafter, to break the will of the landlady by a rigid application of the rule.

The maid began this shuttling system of irrigation
which continued well into the afternoon. Her looks
blackened. After the jam sponge, she came back
flustered and asked if we wanted coffee. One bright
spark asked if it was in a pot.

'We'd rather have it in cups, being as how it's a
boarding house, not a hotel. We wouldn't want to
break the rules,' he replied, as the weary wench went
back to offer her resignation.

                    Russell Harty, *Hols at the Hotel Tralee*, 1980

*How to ease out the unwanted guest is the subject of
this vintage Perelman essay, entitled 'The Customer is
Always Wrong.'*

The National Hotel Exposition is an annual powwow
at which innkeepers forgather to discuss trade secrets:
the maintenance of proper standards of insolence among
room clerks, improved methods of juggling shower
faucets so that guests are alternately frozen and
parboiled, artful techniques for making windows stick,
and the like. The chief topic of the convention, under-
standably, was overcrowding. A variety of speakers
addressed the gathering, analysing the congestion and
suggesting remedies. One delegate from the City of
Brotherly Love came out of his corner snarling. 'The
resident manager of the Warwick Hotel, in Phila-
delphia,' stated the *Times*, 'suggested a more selective
method of meting out rooms ... declaring himself in
favor of the "prestige guest who will be a source of
revenue to the hotel," adding that many long-term
guests who are "meaningless people" were cluttering up
hotels and preventing them from gaining good pros-
pects'. This acid diagnosis was challenged from the
floor by an official of Chicago's Palmer House with the

hot assertion that 'the unimportant guest of today may be the "big shot of tomorrow."'

It so happens that several days ago I was in the lobby of the San Culotte, a rather dusty family hotel in the West Forties. I had gone there to meet a friend with whom I was lunching, when I heard an irate voice behind me.

'Look at this lobby!' it was saying. 'Did you ever see such a pack of crumbs? Of all the inconsequential, meaningless loafers' – I stole a glance over my shoulder and beheld a pursy, apoplectic gentleman, unmistakably the manager, surveying the lounge with arms akimbo. He was addressing a lathlike subordinate in mournful black and rimless bifocals, quite obviously his assistant.

'Shh, Mr Leftwich,' the younger man placated. 'They're all steady guests, except one or two. Been here for years.'

'You bet they have,' snapped his superior. 'That's what's wrong with the San Culotte. I tell you, Rightwich, I've had enough of these measly nonentities lousing up my establishment. I want people that *mean* something – celebrities, d'ye hear? Diplomats, movie stars, suave men of letters!'

'We had a suave man of letters last summer,' reminded Rightwich, 'but he left on account of the roaches.'

'Listen,' grated the manager. 'I put thirteen thousand dollars' worth of roaches into this place to give it a homelike atmosphere, and anybody who doesn't like 'em can start packing!' He moved into my line of vision and indicated a commonplace citizen sleepily engaged in paring his nails. 'Now, take that chump, for instance,' he went on in a lower voice. 'Who is he?'

'That's Mr Detweiler,' replied Rightwich. 'He's an ideal guest. Never missed a bill. Why, he's so prompt –'

'Never mind that,' interrupted Leftwich. 'Promptness don't get you into *Who's Who*. What's he *do*?'

'Well,' hesitated Rightwich, 'he just sort of grooms his nails.'

'You see?' snorted the other, triumphantly. 'Dead wood. What I want is Yul Brynner sitting there grooming his nails, not a cipher named Detweiler. How about the one with the *Racing Form*, by the potted palm?'

'Mr Pfannkuchen?' protested Rightwich, aggrieved. 'Ah, gee, boss, he's gilt-edged – he pays us a year in advance. And he doesn't even ask for a room. He sleeps in a broom closet.'

'He's a bottleneck,' grunted Leftwich inexorably. 'The place is full of 'em. That old lady knitting the afghan there – '

'She's kind of distinguished, though,' appealed the assistant. 'She looks like Dame May Whitty if you close your eyes a little.'

'I'm closing my ears, too,' growled Leftwich. 'Get this straight, now. We're combing the small fry out of the register once and for all.'

'But gosh, Mr Leftwich,' implored the young man. 'You can't tell, one of our guests *might* become famous all of a sudden. Every dog has his day.'

'Just a minute,' rapped the manager, wheeling on him. 'Are you trying to take sides with the clientele?'

'No, no, of course not,' stammered Rightwich, overcome with confusion: 'All I mean is – '

'We've got an ugly name for that in our business, boy.' Leftwich's eyes had narrowed to mere slits. 'It's called taking sides with the clientele.'

The Most of S. J. Perelman, 1959

The Pleasures of the Table

In the nineteenth century, hotels, great and small, began to cater for banquets. These could be almost military in their formal drill, especially in the US.

There will be seen a magnificent set-out dinner-table for a hundred or more guests, with a line of table napkins, in upright fantastic form, stuck into every tumbler, which range along each side of the table, from end to end. The meals – all previously prepared and brought up – are placed on side tables, and there delivered to the white or colored waiters, each one of whom has four or six guests to wait upon. It is one of the most novel sights for a stranger to see in one of these immense dining halls, a whole regiment of Sambos, waiting for the signal to uncover such of the dishes as are placed on the table before the guests. After all the company are seated, say twenty to thirty of these waiters are ranged, one half on each side of the table, behind the guests, in military line. At a given signal, each one reaches over his arm and takes hold of the handle of a dish. That is the first motion. There they all hold for a second or two, when, at another signal, they all at the same moment lift the cover, all as if flying off at one whoop, and with as great exactness as soldiers expected to 'shoulder arms'. This is the case in the $2 and $2.50 houses in the large cities. Even in hotels where the charge is only $1 a day, or $3 or $4 per week, the set-out is not to be despised.

G. H. Baillière, *British American Guide Book*, 1859

In Britain, around the turn of the century, Escoffier reigned supreme, first at the Savoy and later at the Ritz. He and his rivals were forever creating new

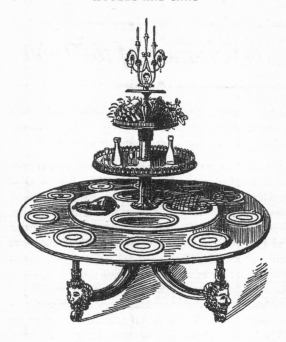

dishes and ever more dazzling presentations for royalty and superstars. With the Prince of Wales, there were special hazards.

The two dishes inseparable from the name of Escoffier in his creative years at the Savoy were *Cuisses de Nymphes à l'Aurore* and *Pêche Melba*, dreamed up for the Prince of Wales and for Mme. Nellie Melba, respectively. The *Nymphes à l'Aurore* created something of a problem of presentation and identification since they were, of course, frogs' legs served cold in a jelly of cream and Moselle tinctured with paprika. The management was afraid, in view of the circumstances at the moment – the Prince was having a flaming affair with Lily Langtry – that gossips might read sardonic intent into the suggestive dish; but it passed off without challenge and everyone in both front office and below stairs breathed easier. If the Prince had detected a suggestion of impropriety in the creation, the Savoy might have been obliged to close its doors then and there.

The peaches for Melba entailed neither such a threat nor such invocation of Escoffier's genius, being nothing more complicated than fresh peaches poached in vanilla syrup served in a timbale on a layer of vanilla ice cream coated with raspberry purée. The initial presentation took place one evening after the diva had sung Elsa in *Lohengrin*, and it was Escoffier's happy conceit to bring the new creation to the table in a magnificent swan carved from a huge block of ice borne by four tottering footmen in knee breeches, to the applause of the entire restaurant. Melba was in ecstasies but Escoffier merely smiled at her delight. To his thinking, mere peaches and ice cream were nothing to get excited about. Unhappily, peach melba is perhaps the most widely imitated and dreadfully libeled of all Escoffier's creations.

Lucius Beebe, *The Savoy of London*, 1963

Few cooks could rise to the gastronomic heights of the Savoy or the Ritz in their heyday – or were as scrupulous in their standards. Fothergill confesses his embarrassment at short-changing two Oxford gourmets.

I had a letter from the Queen's College, asking for an elaborate dinner, for two, each dish was meticulously prescribed; for instance, pheasant (shooting had begun only the day before) without 'bread poultice, gravel or fried counters', and so on. But disliking to have undergraduates spend extravagantly I got ready a very nice meal though I winkled their oysters, so to speak, all the way through: chicken, for instance, instead of gunwarm pheasant, and for aubergines stuffed cucumber. They arrived and weren't undergraduates at all, but, as I learnt afterwards, T. W. Allen, Fellow of Queen's College, and Dr Cowley, Curator of the Bodleian, the two undisputed reigning epicures of Oxford. Allen had, at least, his bottle of Château d'Yquem 1914, and 'Cowles' his Château Lafite 1907. After dinner, said Allen heavily: 'We are a dining club, we've dined together for twenty-five years. Once we had a guest, but never again. This is the first time we've dined out of College, but we shall return.' They never did. I couldn't tell them the reason why I had economized, I was so sick about it all. Anyhow Dr Cowley, at least, got knighted later.

John Fothergill, *An Innkeeper's Diary*, 1931

One of the pleasures of staying at a good hotel is the opportunity to gorge oneself on wonderful food. Hotels often pander to their guests' appetites, though few as generously as the famous Sharrow Bay Hotel on Ulls-water in the English Lakes.

Sharrow Bay Hotel
Ullswater
Tuesday

Dear Doctor Goldstuck,

You probably won't remember but I came to your clinic last week to talk about your famous high protein diet. You said I didn't need to lose weight and only under protest gave me two appetite suppressants, pink I think, in a little glass bottle, just to see what they tasted like. Any chance of your sending me up another couple of dozen by Red Star parcel to Penrith, *sharpish* because two appetite suppressants in this place is a bit like taking an extra cardy up Mount Everest.

Have you heard about it? You should. I swear if you moved your clinic from Wimpole Street to Pooley Bridge you'd make your fortune – well, your *second* fortune. I'll tell you about it while waiting for lunch.

Seven years ago it won the Egon Ronay Hotel of the Year award and this year it got his Restaurant of the Year award, which makes it the only place in Britain to bag both. It's run by two charming gentlemen, Francis and Brian. Francis cooks, Brian greets and every spare moment that they're not cooking or greeting or meeting the overnight train from London with their fresh *mange-tout* they're scouring the antique shops of Cumbria for bric-a-brac to deck their hotel with.

The whole place is stiff with cherubs and teapots and chiming clocks and bowls of pot pourri and button-back chairs and occasional tables. Pink is the predominant colour, mimosa the pervading fragrance, velvet the preferred texture. I keep wanting to open the windows. Is this what they mean by summer camp?

My bedroom is like the eighteenth-century furniture saleroom of Christie's on viewing day. I haven't tried swinging a cat in it yet, but I need a chart to navigate between the wardrobe and the window seat. There are frills on the dressing table; flounces on the headboard and a pink velvet ribbon round the aerosol room spray (rose fragrance). The soap is flower-shaped, the coat-hangers have lavender bags tied to them with satin ribbons, the light switches are green silk tassels and, until I hastily improvised a valance out of two candy pink and white hand towels (theirs) and a pair of frilly knickers (mine) to gird its nether quarters, the trouser press looked quite *rude*. Having downed my welcoming glass of sherry and wolfed the petits fours in my bedside biscuit tin, I descended to the lounge overlooking the lake for afternoon tea.

Oh, Dr Goldstuck, where were you when I needed you? I had whisper-thin egg and cress and ham and chicken and tomato sandwiches followed not so much by a selection from the cake stand as by every item on the cake stand. It was irresistible. Strawberry tartlets fashioned like wicker sewing baskets, their lids propped open with dollops of cream; plum cake whose dusky benisons burst against my palate like bubbles of swollen sweetness; fudge fingers and madeira and shortbread and madeleines.

'No, Jean dear, I won't' said a woman nearby. 'Remember there's a seven-course dinner coming up.' Heavy hearted and heavier bellied, I staggered into the spectacular lakeside garden to drum up an appetite with a feeble attempt at exercise. At eight the dinner gong sounded and, like so many innocents to the slaughter, we were shown into the dining room.

There were seventy-seven separate items on the menu. I vaguely remember eating smoked salmon stuffed with something, coated with something else and garnished with a bright pink rhododendron florette, but so befuddled were my taste-buds and bedevilled my brain by the half way stage – lemon sorbet between the turbot and the lamb – that it might easily have been stuffed cherub coated with pot pourri and garnished with a lavender bag. The guests ate mainly in silence emitting occasional squeals of delight or groans of ecstasy. Soft-footed waiters hovered murmuring constantly, reassuringly, 'Everything all right, Madam?'

By the time I reached the Olde English Regency Syllabub As Presented by Francis At Maxim's I was feeling giddy. Last night I dreamt I drowned in chocolate Bavarois.

Morning at last, and the agony continues. A five-course breakfast, scalloped apple rings with the bacon, croissants like great golden lobsters, figs, peaches ... Must stop. Morning coffee and Danish pastries are being served next door. I may be mistaken, but the cherub holding up the light on the grand piano seems to have put on a bit of weight since last night. Don't forget the pills.

Yours fully,

Sue

Sue Arnold, *Glutton-backed Chairs and Cherubs*, 1981

The enjoyment of eating depends as much on the right company as on the cooking. It is hard to appreciate one's dinner if one is eating alone, even harder if there are solitary diners at all the other tables. Such a meal is recorded by Christopher Wiseman in his poem 'Hotel Dining Room, London'.

I count sixteen others scattered
In this room for dinner. All men,
All alone. Not a woman or child.
Separate tables and total silence
Except for the quick soft rattling
Of one man's evening paper, the
Sudden self-conscious clack of utensils.
The occasional waiter ghosts past me.

There's a Frenchman, an American,
A balding man from Lancashire.
This I know from hearing them order.
The others are too far away,
Floating in still pools of isolation.
One has an impressive Guards tie,
Or something like it, and the best
Suit in the room. Another one
Looks as if he's here to haunt
The British Museum, his corduroy
Jacket human and reassuring.
But even he won't meet my eye.

In the high room we eat steadily.
The silence is strange, muffled
And enclosing, as if the place had been
Built to keep the world right out.
We sit like specimens under glass,
And I wonder just who they all are,
If they are moving from or towards
Something, if their reasons for being
Here are crucial or casual, if they
Have families round other tables.
It would be good to talk to them.

No matter. I'll forget their faces.
But I'll remember this quiet evening,
Some people brought for an hour into
My life for me to wonder about before

Memory releases them to float
Away like charred and wind-blown paper.

Meanwhile we eat. We are alone
At this odd junction of time and place,
Strangers at the hub of Empire.

I catch an eye and quickly look away.

Christopher Wiseman, *The Upper Hand*, 1981

The insolence of waiters, especially in the more opulent kind of establishment, has often been commented upon. One of the more famous scenes in the literature of hotels occurs in the following episode from Arnold Bennett's Grand Babylon Hotel. The denouement of this incident, in the succeeding chapter, is Racksole's instant purchase of the Grand Babylon and the abrupt come-uppance of the egregious Jules.

'Yes, sir?'

Jules, the celebrated head waiter of the Grand Babylon, was bending formally towards the alert, middle-aged man who had just entered the smoking-room and dropped into a basket-chair in the corner by the conservatory. It was 7.45 on a particularly sultry

June night, and dinner was about to be served at the Grand Babylon. Men of all sizes, ages, and nationalities, but every one alike arrayed in faultless evening dress, were dotted about the large, dim apartment. A faint odour of flowers came from the conservatory, and the tinkle of a fountain. The waiters, commanded by Jules, moved softly across the thick Oriental rugs, balancing their trays with the dexterity of jugglers, and receiving and executing orders with that air of profound importance of which only really first-class waiters have the secret. The atmosphere was an atmosphere of serenity and repose, characteristic of the Grand Babylon. It seemed impossible that anything could occur to mar the peaceful, aristocratic monotony of existence in that perfectly-managed establishment. Yet on that night was to happen the mightiest upheaval that the Grand Babylon had ever known.

'Yes, sir?' repeated Jules, and this time there was a shade of august disapproval in his voice: it was not usual for him to have to address a customer twice.

'Oh!' said the alert, middle-aged man, looking up at length. Beautifully ignorant of the identity of the great Jules, he allowed his grey eyes to twinkle as he caught sight of the expression on the waiter's face. 'Bring me an Angel Kiss.'

'Pardon, sir?'

'Bring me an Angel Kiss, and be good enough to lose no time.'

'If it's an American drink, I fear we don't keep it, sir.' The voice of Jules fell icily distinct, and several men glanced round uneasily, as if to deprecate the slightest disturbance of their calm. The appearance of the person to whom Jules was speaking, however, reassured them somewhat, for he had all the look of that expert, the travelled Englishman, who can differentiate between one hotel and another by instinct, and who knows at once where he may make a fuss with propriety, and where it is advisable to behave exactly as at the club. The Grand Babylon was a hotel in whose smoking-room one behaved as though one was at one's club.

'I didn't suppose you did keep it, but you can mix it, I guess, even in this hotel.'

'This isn't an American hotel, sir.' The calculated insolence of the words was cleverly masked beneath an accent of humble submission.

The alert, middle-aged man sat up straight, and gazed placidly at Jules, who was pulling his famous red side-whiskers.

'Get a liqueur glass,' he said, half curtly and half with good-humoured tolerance, 'pour into it equal quantities of maraschino, cream, and crème de menthe. Don't stir it; don't shake it. Bring it to me. And, I say, tell the bar-tender –'

'Bar-tender, sir?'

'Tell the bar-tender to make a note of the recipe, as I shall probably want an Angel Kiss every evening before dinner so long as this weather lasts.'

'I will send the drink to you, sir,' said Jules distantly. That was his parting shot, by which he indicated that he was not as other waiters are, and that any person who treated him with disrespect did so at his own peril.

Arnold Bennett, *The Grand Babylon Hotel*, 1902

Carnal Encounters

The ancient, true and proper use of Inns, Ale Houses and Victualling Houses is for the Receipt, Relief and Lodging of Wayfaring People travelling from place to place and not meant for the entertaining and harbouring of Lewd and Idle People to spend and consume their Money and Time in Lewd and Drunken Manner.

Act of Parliament, 1604

Notwithstanding Acts of Parliament, hotels have often served other purposes than simply providing guests with a night's rest. Boswell in his London Journal *describes with the utmost satisfaction his conquest of Louisa at the Black Lion off Fleet Street. (A few days after this episode, he reports ruefully his having caught the pox of the lady.)*

I bethought me of a place to which Louisa and I might safely go. I went to my good friend Hayward's at the Black Lion, told him that I had married, and that I and my wife, who was to be in town on Saturday, would sleep in his house till I got a lodging for her. The King of Prussia says in one of his poems that gallantry comprises every vice. That of lying it certainly does, without which intrigue can never be carried on. But as the proverb says, in love and war all is fair. I who am a lover and hope to be a soldier think so. In this instance we could not be admitted to any decent house except as man and wife. Indeed, we are so if union of hearts be the principal requisite. We are so, at least for a time.

At the appointed hour of eight I went to the Piazzas, where I sauntered up and down for a while in a sort of trembling suspense, I knew not why. At last my

charming companion appeared, and I immediately conducted her to a hackney-coach which I had ready
waiting, pulled up the blinds, and away we drove to
the destined scene of delight. We contrived to seem as
if we had come off a journey, and carried in a bundle
our night-clothes, handkerchiefs, and other little things.
We also had with us some almond biscuits, or as they
call them in London, macaroons, which looked like
provision on the road. On our arrival at Hayward's we
were shown into the parlour, in the same manner that
any decent couple would be. I here thought proper
to conceal my own name (which the people of the
house had never heard), and assumed the name of
Mr Digges.

We supped cheerfully and agreeably and drank a few
glasses, and then the maid came and put the sheets,
well aired, upon the bed. I now contemplated my fair
prize. Louisa is just twenty-four, of a tall rather than
short figure, finely made in person, with a handsome
face and an enchanting languish in her eyes. She
dresses with taste. She has sense, good humour, and
vivacity, and looks quite a woman in genteel life. As
I mused on this elevating subject, I could not help
being somehow pleasingly confounded to think that
so fine a woman was at this moment in my possession,
that without any motives of interest she had come with
me to an inn, agreed to be my intimate companion, as
to be my bedfellow all night, and to permit me the
full enjoyment of her person.

When the servant left the room, I embraced her
warmly and begged that she would not now delay my
felicity. She declined to undress before me, and begged
I would retire and send her one of the maids. I did
so, gravely desiring the girl to go up to Mrs Digges.
I then took a candle in my hand and walked out to
the yard. The night was very dark and very cold. I
experienced for some minutes the rigours of the season,
and called into my mind many terrible ideas of hard-
ships, that I might make a transition from such dreary

thoughts to the most gay and delicious feelings. I then caused make a bowl of negus, very rich of the fruit, which I caused be set in the room as a reviving cordial.

I came softly into the room, and in a sweet delirium slipped into bed and was immediately clasped in her snowy arms and pressed to her milk-white bosom. Good heavens, what a loose did we give to amorous dalliance! The friendly curtain of darkness concealed our blushes. In a moment I felt myself animated with the strongest powers of love, and, from my dearest creature's kindness, had a most luscious feast. Proud of my godlike vigour, I soon resumed the noble game. I was in full glow of health. Sobriety had preserved me from effeminacy and weakness, and my bounding blood beat quick and high alarms. A more voluptuous night I never enjoyed. Five times was I fairly lost in supreme rapture. Louisa was madly fond of me; she declared I was a prodigy, and asked me if this was not extraordinary for human nature. I said twice as much might be, but this was not, although in my own mind I was somewhat proud of my performance. She said it was what there was no just reason to be proud of. But I told her I could not help it. She said it was what we had in common with the beasts. I said no. For we had it highly improved by the pleasures of sentiment. I asked her what she thought enough. She gently chid me for asking such questions, but said two times.

She often insisted that we should compose ourselves to sleep before I would consent to it. At last I sunk to

rest in her arms and she in mine. I found the negus,
which had a fine flavour, very refreshing to me. Louisa
had an exquisite mixture of delicacy and wantonness
that made me enjoy her with more relish. Indeed I
could not help roving in fancy to the embraces of some
other ladies which my lively imagination strongly
pictured. I don't know if that was altogether fair.
However, Louisa had all the advantage. She said she
was quite fatigued and could neither stir leg nor arm.
She begged I would not despise her, and hoped my love
would not be altogether transient. I have painted this
night as well as I could. The description is faint; but I
surely may be styled a Man of Pleasure.

THURSDAY 13 JANUARY. We awaked from sweet
repose after the luscious fatigues of the night. I got up
between nine and ten and walked out till Louisa should
rise. I then came in and we had an agreeable breakfast,
after which we left Hayward's, who said he was sorry
he had not more of our company, and calling a hackney-
coach, drove to Soho Square, where Louisa had some
visits to pay. So we parted. I really conducted this
affair with a manliness and prudence that pleased me
very much. The whole expense was just eighteen
shillings.

James Boswell, A *London Journal*, 1763

*Not all beaux' stratagems are successful. Casanova's
intentions were frustrated when he visited the Star
Tavern, London.*

I went to dine at the 'Star' Tavern, where I had been
told that the prettiest and choicest girls in London
were to be found. I enter the tavern, I ask a waiter
for a private room. The host, observing that I do not
speak English, addresses me in French, sits down with
me, orders what I want, and I am so surprised by his
polite, grave, and solemn manner that I cannot pluck
up courage to tell him that I want to dine with a
pretty English girl. I finally tell him in a roundabout
way that I do not know if Lord Pembroke has deceived

me in saying that I could have the prettiest girls in London there.

'No, Monsieur, he did not deceive you, and if that is what you want you can have as many as you please.'

He calls 'Waiter', whereupon a neat young man appears, whom he orders to send a girl for my service, as if he were ordering him to bring me paper and ink. The waiter leaves, and ten minutes later in comes a girl, whose appearance I dislike. I tell the host plainly that she does not please me.

'Give a shilling for the chairmen, and send her away. No one stands on ceremony in London, Monsieur.'

I order the shilling given, and I ask for another girl, but a pretty one. The second arrives, worse than the first. I send her away. I also send away the third, the fourth, the fifth, and so on up to the tenth, delighted to see that, far from displeasing the host, my fastidiousness amuses him. I say I want no more girls, I want to dine; but I tell him I am sure the waiter had been making game of me to please the chairmen.

'That may be so, Monsieur; they always do it when they are not told the name and address of the girl who is wanted.'

Casanova (1725–98), *History of My Life*

Young gentlemen on the Grand Tour expected to have amatory adventures en route if their tutor allowed. Some indication of the morals of the day is shown by a guide book, published in 1822, with useful phrases and dialogues provided in French, German, and Italian. One section is entitled 'At the Inn', and contains a conversation between a Tourist, an innkeeper and a chambermaid named Joan.

'God keep you from misfortune, my host!'
'You are welcome, Gentlemen!'
'Shall we be well lodged with you for this night?'
'Yes, very well, Sir.'

'Have you good stable, good hay, good oats, good litter, good wine?'

'The best ...'

[*The Tourist alights with his companions and enters the inn where he drinks too heavily with his meal.*]

'By your leaves, Gentlemen, I find myself somewhat indispos'd.'

'Sir, if you are not well, go take your rest, your chamber is ready. Joan, make a good fire in his chamber, and let him want for nothing.'

'Sweetheart, is my bed made? Is it good, clean warm?'

'Yes, Sir, it is a good featherbed. The sheets are very clean.'

'Pull off my stockings, and warm my bed, for I am much out of order. I shake like a leaf in a tree. Warm a Napkin for my head and bind it well. Gently, you bind it too hard. Bring my pillow, and cover me well; draw the curtains, and pin them together. Where is the chamber-pot? Where is the privy?'

'Follow me and I will show you the way. Go strait up and you will find it on your right hand; if you see it not you will soon smell it. Sir, do you want anything else?'

'Yes, my dear, put out the candle and come nearer to me.'

'I will put it out when I am out of the room; what is your will? Are you not well enough yet?'

'My head lies too low, raise up the bolster a little. I cannot lie so low. My dear, give me a kiss, I should sleep the better.'

'You are not sick since you talk of kissing. I would rather die than kiss a man in his bed, or any other place. Take your rest in God's name. God give you a good night and good rest.'

'I thank you, fair maid.'

The Gentleman's Pocket Companion for Travelling into Foreign Parts, 1722

and full of good juice. She felt happy that part of her body was occupied by someone else. The spirit of the white hotel was against selfishness.

D. M. Thomas, *The White Hotel*, 1981

Daisy Ashford wrote The Young Visiters *in 1919 at the age of nine. There is certainly nothing explicitly sexual in the following scene, though the air is heavy with innocent innuendoes.*

BERNARDS IDEAR

After Mr Salteena had departed Bernard Clark thourght he would show Ethel over his house so they spent a merry morning so doing. Ethel passed bright remarks on all the rooms and Bernard thourght she was most pretty and Ethel began to be a bit excited. After a lovly lunch they sat in the gloomy hall and Ethel began to feel very glad Mr Salteena was not there. Suddenly Bernard lit his pipe I was thinking he said passionately what about going up to London for a weeks Gaierty.

Who inquired Ethel in a low tone.

You and me said Bernard I know of several splendid hotels and we could go to theaters and parties and enjoy ourselves to the full.

So we could what an idear cried Ethel.

So the merry plan was all arranged ...

Arrived in the gay city Bernard hailed a cab to the manner born and got in followed by Ethel. Kindly drive us to the Gaierty Hotel he cried in a firm tone. The cab-man waved his whip and off they dashed.

We shall be highly comfortable and select at the Gaierty said Bernard and he thourght to himself how lovly it would be if he was married to Ethel. He blushed a deep shade at his own thourghts and gave a side long glance at Ethel who was gazing out of the window. Well one never knows he murmered to himself and as one of the poets says great events from trivil causes springs.

Just then they stopped at the gay hotel and Ethel was spellbound at the size of the big hall – Bernard poked his head into the window of the pay desk. Have you a coupple of bedrooms for self and young lady he enquired in a lordly way.

A very handsome lady with golden hair and a lace apron glanced at a book and hastily replied Oh yes sir two beauties on the 1st floor number 9 and 10.

Thankyou said Bernard we will go up if you have no objection.

None whatever sir said the genial lady the beds are well aired and the view is quite pleasant.

Come along Ethel cried Bernard this sounds alright eh.

Oh quite said Ethel with a beaming smile.

They went upstairs and entered number 9 a very fine compartment with a large douny bed and white doors with glass handles leading into number 10 and equally dainty room but a trifle smaller.

Which will you have Ethel asked Bernard.

Oh well I would rarther you settled it said Ethel. I am willing to abide by your choice.

The best shall be yours then said Bernard bowing gallantly and pointing to the biggest room.

Ethel blushed at his speaking look. I shall be quite lost in that huge bed she added to hide her embarrassment.

Yes I expect you will said Bernard and now what about a little table d'ote followed by a theater.

Oh yes cried Ethel and downstairs they went.

Daisy Ashford, *The Young Visiters*, 1919

Misadventures & Misunderstandings

Many criminals have been arrested in hotels; 'Two gentlemen to see you, Sir', has indeed become a catchphrase for these episodes. A notable hotel arrest was that of Oscar Wilde at the Cadogan Hotel, London, immortalized in this poem by John Betjeman.

He sipped at a weak hock and seltzer
   As he gazed at the London skies
Through the Nottingham lace of the curtains
   Or was it his bees-winged eyes?

To the right and before him Pont Street
   Did tower in her new-built red,
As hard as the morning gaslight
   That shone on his unmade bed,

'I want some more hock in my seltzer,
   And Robbie, please give me your hand –
Is this the end or beginning?
   How can I understand?

'So you've brought me the latest *Yellow Book*:
   And Buchan has got in it now:
Approval of what is approved of
   Is as false as a well-kept vow.

'More hock, Robbie – where is the seltzer?
   Dear boy, pull again at the bell!
They are all little better than *cretins*,
   Though this *is* the Cadogan Hotel.

'One astrakhan coat is at Willis's –
   Another one's at the Savoy:

Do fetch my morocco portmanteau,
    And bring them on later, dear boy.'

A thump, and a murmur of voices –
    ('Oh why must they make such a din?')
As the door of the bedroom swung open
    And TWO PLAIN-CLOTHES POLICEMEN came in:

'Mr Woilde, we 'ave come for tew take yew
    Where felons and criminals dwell:
We must ask yew tew leave with us quoietly
    For this is the Cadogan Hotel.'

He rose, and he put down *The Yellow Book.*
    He staggered – and, terrible-eyed,
He brushed past the palms on the staircase
    And was helped to a hansom outside.

> John Betjeman, 'The Arrest of Oscar Wilde at the
> Cadogan Hotel', 1948

Inns have often been the scene of ugly brawls. One of the more bizarre punch-ups in history took place in the lounge of the Orpheus Ascending Inn in Stockbridge, Massachusetts, when a drunk abused Norman Mailer's fifth wife, the cabaret singer Carol Stevens.

Carol Mailer is one of the most beautiful women I have ever known, tall, with well-chiseled bones and enormous black eyes which are deep and compassionate. She also possesses a full-throated, warm, blues-singing voice. As Carol Stevens she had made recordings and sung in clubs, but she had been inactive for a number of years. One day as Steve and I sat with Norman and Carol over a bottle of Pott's rum, we discussed the idea of Carol Stevens singing on Friday nights at Orpheus. Carol's eloquent eyes grew enormous with expectation.

We all decided that the sooner she began singing at the inn the better. Carol worked hard on her repertoire while Steve advertised that Miss Carol Stevens was to open in cabaret at Orpheus Ascending two weeks from that Friday.

Opening night in she swept, wearing a magnificent bright green chiffon gown, yards and yards of flowing fabric attached to glittering rhinestone clips at the shoulders of the dress. The gels had been changed to give a soft blue stage light, and the room beyond was made even darker than usual. Carol stood majestically at the microphone, her dark hair piled into a Grecian crown on her head. Norman sat at one of the window banquettes which offered the best view of Carol. The adjoining banquette was occupied by two couples who were strangers to Orpheus. They had been drinking heavily and were noisy and extremely high-spirited.

Carol began her first number. Norman leaned over and politely asked the man seated closest to him to be quiet. The man ignored him. Norman bristled, drew back, but all the while Carol was singing it was obvious the strangers were straining his tolerance level. Halfway through Carol's third number, the man nearest Norman turned away from his companions and called out, 'Is that broad stacked!'

'Be quiet,' Norman ordered.

'Sex-y!' the man continued.

With that Norman turned to face the stranger, grabbed him by the ears and in a split moment had butted his own head so hard against the man's head that there was a resounding *craaaaack!* The stranger was holding his head and moaning. Norman had turned back to watch Carol. She was a ghostly sight, unable to conceal the fear in her eyes as she raised the decibel level of her voice.

'That old man nearly cracked my skull,' shouted the stranger, pointing to Norman's tousled gray head.

Norman rose to his feet and pushed the table back. 'I challenge you to a re-butt,' he said.

Carol stopped singing. The two men stepped out into the narrow aisle between tables. Steve came running, pushing himself between them. 'The house will buy everyone drinks in the bar,' he said, sweating.

I thought, 'My God, he'll get hurt standing between

those two!' I pushed my chair back, stumbled to my feet, reached up and grabbed Norman's arm. 'Remember, Norman,' I said inanely, not able to think of anything else, 'this isn't just a supper club, it is also my home.'

Norman suspended his challenging glance as he turned to me. I held my breath. Carol was behind me. 'If you do this, Norman,' she said over my shoulder, 'I'll never forgive you.' She began to cry and I turned and held her against my shoulder.

'We'll go outside,' Norman decided, as the stranger let out a string of abusive remarks and curses.

Steffi, Joan Mills and I took Carol upstairs. 'Someday,' Carol cried, 'someone will have a knife. Maybe that crazy man he challenged has one.' She was terrified, angry and inconsolable. 'Go down and see what's happening,' she begged. 'It's too quiet. I can't stand it.'

There was no one in the lounge. I walked into the bar. It was jammed with people. Standing in the center were Norman and the stranger, no longer a stranger, bear-hugging, toasting each other.

'You have a hard head,' Norman said admiringly.

'Yours is pretty tough for an old man,' admitted Norman's new friend. Steve later explained that the man had met Norman in a re-butt and been able to remain on his feet, thereby gaining Norman's sincere respect.

Anne Edwards and Steven Citron, *The Inn and Us*, 1976

[82]

Sir Ronald Storrs, in his memoirs, Orientations, *describes another outlandish episode which took place on the terrace of Shepheard's Hotel, Cairo, in 1907. The instigator on this occasion was the eccentric Oriental Secretary at the British Embassy, Harry Boyle.*

He was extremely well read, especially in English and French eighteenth-century literature, an exquisite precisian in language and a perennially amusing conversationalist. On most afternoons he walked abroad, dressed with a distinguished improbability. His coat was old, his trousers bagged at the knee and sagged at the waist, his boots were almost mediaeval in their turn up. On his head a battered straw hat; rather beyond heel a mongrel but *sympathique* cur: the whole enclosing a man of genius. This very appearance was the occasion of a triumph of resource.

He was taking his tea one day on the terrace of Shepheard's Hotel when he heard himself accosted by a total stranger: 'Sir, are you the Hotel Pimp?' 'I am, Sir,' Boyle replied without hesitation or emotion, 'but the management, as you may observe, are good enough to allow me the hour of five to six as a tea interval. If, however, you are pressed, perhaps you will address yourself to that gentleman,' and he indicated Sir Thomas Lipton, 'who is taking my duty; you will find him most willing to accommodate you in any little commissions of a confidential character which you may see fit to entrust to him.' Boyle then paid his bill, and stepped into a cab unobtrusively, but not too quickly to hear the sound of a fracas, the impact of a fist and the thud of a ponderous body on the marble floor.

Ronald Storrs, *Orientations*, 1937

The comic and farcical possibilities inherent in hotel life have often been realized in the theatre. One of the more famous of such scenes occurs in the second act of Goldsmith's She Stoops to Conquer. *Hastings and Marlow are to stay with Mr Hardcastle whom they*

[83]

have never met. They lose their way and are directed by the mischievous Tony Lumpkin to Mr Hardcastle's house but believe that they have been sent to an inn.

SERVANT. Welcome, gentlemen, very welcome. This way.

HASTINGS. Upon my word, a very well-looking house; antique, but creditable.

MARLOW. The usual fate of a large mansion. Having first ruined the master by good housekeeping, it at last comes to levy contributions as an inn.

HASTINGS. As you say, we passengers are to be taxed to pay all these fineries. I have often seen a good sideboard, or a marble chimneypiece, though not actually put in the bill, inflame a reckoning confoundedly.

MARLOW. Travellers, George, must pay in all places. The only difference is, that in good inns, you pay dearly for luxuries; in bad ones, you are fleeced and starved.

Shortly afterwards, Mr Hardcastle himself arrives to make them welcome. His guests demand to know what is for supper.

HARDCASTLE. For supper, sir! (*Aside*) Was ever such a request to a man in his own house!

MARLOW. Yes, sir, supper sir; I begin to feel an appetite. I shall make devilish work tonight in the larder, I promise you.

HARDCASTLE. (*Aside*). Such a brazen dog sure never my eyes beheld. (*To him*) Why really, sir, as for supper I can't well tell. My Dorothy, and the cook-maid, settle these things between them. I leave these kind of things entirely to them.

MARLOW. You do, do you?

HARDCASTLE. Entirely. By the bye, I believe they are in actual consultation upon what's for supper this moment in the kitchen.

MARLOW. Then I beg they'll admit *me* as one of their

privy council. It's a way I have got. When I travel, I always choose to regulate my own supper. Let the cook be called. No offence, I hope, sir.

HARDCASTLE. O no, sir, none in the least; yet I don't know how: our Bridget, the cook-maid, is not very communicative upon these occasions. Should we send for her, she might scold us all out of the house.

HASTINGS. Let's see your list of the larder then. I ask it as a favour. I always match my appetite to my bill of fare.

MARLOW (*To* HARDCASTLE, *who looks at them with surprise*). Sir, he's very right, and it's my way too.

HARDCASTLE. Sir, you have a right to command here. Here, Roger, bring us the bill of fare for tonight's supper. I believe it's drawn out. Your manner, Mr Hastings, puts me in mind of my uncle, Colonel Wallop. It was a saying of his, that no man was sure of his supper till he had eaten it.

Enter ROGER, *who gives a Bill of Fare*

HASTINGS (*Aside*). All upon the high ropes! His uncle a Colonel! We shall soon hear of his mother being a Justice of Peace. But let's hear the bill of fare.

MARLOW (*Perusing*). What's here? For the first course; for the second course; for the dessert. The devil, sir, do you think we have brought down the whole Joiners Company, or the Corporation of Bedford, to eat up such a supper? Two or three little things, clean and comfortable, will do.

HASTINGS. But, let's hear it.

MARLOW (*Reading*). For the first course at the top, a pig's face, and prune sauce.

HASTINGS. Damn your pig's face, I say.

MARLOW. And damn your prune sauce, say I.

HARDCASTLE. And yet, gentlemen, to men that are hungry, a pig's face, with prune sauce, is very good eating.

MARLOW. At the bottom, a calf's tongue and brains.

HASTINGS. Let your brains be knocked out, my good sir; I don't like them.

MARLOW. Or you may clap them on a plate by themselves. I do.

HARDCASTLE (*Aside*). Their impudence confounds me. (*To them*) Gentlemen, you are my guests, make what alterations you please. Is there anything else you wish to retrench or alter, gentlemen?

MARLOW. Item. A pork pie, a boiled rabbit and sausages, a florentine, a shaking pudding, and a dish of tiff-tuff-taffety cream!

HASTINGS. Confound your made dishes, I shall be as much at a loss in this house as at a green and yellow dinner at the French ambassador's table. I'm for plain eating.

HARDCASTLE. I'm sorry, gentlemen, that I have nothing you like, but if there be anything you have a particular fancy to –

MARLOW. Why, really, sir, your bill of fare is so exquisite, that any one part of it is full as good as another. Send us what you please. So much for supper. And now to see that our beds are aired, and properly taken care of.

HARDCASTLE. I entreat you'll leave all that to me. You shall not stir a step.

MARLOW. Leave that to you! I protest, sir, you must excuse me, I always look to these things myself.

HARDCASTLE. I must insist, sir, you'll make yourself easy on that head.

MARLOW. You see I'm resolved on it. (*Aside*) A very troublesome fellow this, as ever I met with.

HARDCASTLE. Well, sir, I'm resolved at least to attend you. (*Aside*) This may be modern modesty, but I never saw anything look so like old-fashioned impudence.

Oliver Goldsmith, *She Stoops to Conquer*, 1773

The hotel as a backdrop for farce achieved a kind of apotheosis in the Fawlty Towers *series on television. In this scene, the Manager, Basil Fawlty, is grovelling when he discovers that a new guest is a Lord. (Later –*

naturellement, as he would say – he finds that the distinguished stranger is in fact a notorious hotel con-man and thief.)

IN RECEPTION
Basil hurries bad-temperedly into the lobby. A distinguished looking gentleman is standing there. He is called Melbury.

BASIL. Yes, yes, well yes?
The new visitor is slightly thrown by the force of this attack.

MELBURY. Er, well, I was wondering if you could offer me accommodation for a few nights?

BASIL (*very cross*). Have you booked?

MELBURY. I'm sorry?

BASIL. Have you booked, have you booked?

MELBURY. No.

BASIL (*to himself*). Oh dear!
He goes behind the desk.

MELBURY. Why, are you full?

BASIL. Oh, we're not full ... We're not *full* ... Of course we're not *full!!*

MELBURY. I'd like er ...

BASIL (*rudely*). One moment, please.
Soon Basil is ready.

BASIL. Yes?

MELBURY. A single room with a ...

BASIL. Your *name* please, could I have your name?

MELBURY. Melbury.
The phone rings. Basil picks it up and gestures Melbury not to interrupt him.

BASIL (*To Melbury*). One second please.

BASIL (*To phone*). Hello? ... Ah yes Mr O'Reilly, well, it's very simple really. When I asked you to build me a wall I was rather hoping that instead of just dumping the bricks in a pile you might have found time to cement them together ... you know, one on top of the other in the traditional fashion.

BASIL (*To Melbury, testily*). Could you fill it in

please? (*To phone*) ... Oh splendid! When? Yes, I know Mr O'Reilly but when?

Melbury is having difficulty with the register. Basil points a finger.

BASIL (*To Melbury*). There, *there*! (*To phone*) Yes but when? Yes, yes, aah! ... the flu! (*To Melbury*) Both names please. (*To phone*) Yes, I should have guessed, yes, flu and the Potato Famine no doubt ...

MELBURY. I beg your pardon?

BASIL. Would you put *both* your names please ... (*to phone*) Well will you give me a *date*?

MELBURY. Er ... I only use one.

BASIL (*with a withering look*). You don't have a first name?

MELBURY. I am *Lord* Melbury ... so I sign myself Melbury.

There is a long, long pause.

BASIL (*to phone*). Go away.

Basil puts the phone down.

BASIL. I'm *so* sorry to have kept you waiting, your lordship ... *please* forgive me. Now, was there something, is there something, anything, I can do for you? Anything ... at all?

MELBURY. Well, I have filled this in ...

BASIL. Oh, don't bother with that please.

He takes the registration form and tosses it away.

BASIL. Now, a special room ... a single? A double? A suite? Well we don't have any suites, but we have some beautiful doubles with a view ...

MELBURY. No, no just a single.

BASIL. Just a single! Absolutely! How very *wise* if I may say so, your honour.

MELBURY. With a bath.

BASIL. Naturally, naturally! *Naturellement!*

He roars with laughter.

MELBURY. I shall be staying for ...

BASIL. Oh please! Please! ... Manuel!!

He bangs the bell. Nothing happens.

BASIL. Well, it's ... it's rather grey today, isn't it?

MELBURY. Oh yes, it is rather.

BASIL. Usually it's quite beautiful down here, but today is a real old ... er ... rotter ... Manuel!!!
Another bang on the bell.

BASIL. Still ... it's good for the wheat.

MELBURY. Yes, er, I suppose so.

BASIL. Oh yes! I hear it's coming along wonderfully at the moment! Thank God! Oh I love the wheat ... there's no sight like a field of wheat waving in the ... waving in the ... *Manuel!!!*

John Cleese and Connie Booth, *Fawlty Towers,* 1979

Accidentally dropping an olive-stone into a guest's soup – the subject of the next mishap – would be an everyday incident with Fawlty Towers's banana-skin Spanish waiter, Manuel – though Manuel would not have carried off the occasion with the aplomb of the maître d'hôtel at Bemelmans' Hotel Splendide.

All maîtres d'hôtel love to eat. They lean over sideboards, behind high screens, to stuff something quickly away. They are especially fond of little fried things which they can pick up from hot dishes as the commis bring them up from the kitchen, such easily disposed-of things as whitebait, oyster crabs, fried scallops, frogs's legs, and fried potatoes. They have learned to eat so that their cheeks and and jaws do not move; they can eat in the middle of the dining-room and no one knows it.

One of the maîtres d'hôtel in the Splendide, a very good-looking one, had a front tooth missing, it was being repaired. At one very busy luncheon he took a green olive from a tray behind the screen on one of his service tables. Just then he was called to a table; the publisher Frank Munsey wanted to order the rest of his luncheon while he waited for his soup to cool. Mr Munsey looked over the card that was handed him and decided on some tête de veau en tortue. As the maître d'hôtel repeated this, with its many T's, the

olive pit shot out through the hole in his teeth and landed in Mr Munsey's soup.

Fortunately the publisher was bent over talking to someone at the next table and saw nothing. The maître d'hôtel nervously asked if he could not take the soup back and get something hotter, but Mr Munsey, a very much feared guest, said he had been waiting for it to cool, it was just about right now.

But there is a way out of such difficulties, a technique of upset and confusion, often employed in dangerous situations with hard clients. The maître d'hôtel first instructs the chef de rang and the commis; there is a small quick meeting – then excitement, noise, shouting, a waving in the face of bills of fare, some pushing, and one, two, three, the soup is gone. All this happens while the maître d'hôtel is a few tables away, so that the client can call him to complain. He comes, is surprised, and calls the waiter names:

'Specimen of an idiot, where is the soup of Monsieur Munsey?'

'Ah, pardon – I thought –' 'You should not think, stupid one! Ah, Monsieur Munsey, pardon, pardon.' The soup is back on the table after the commis, behind the screen, has fished the olive pit out with his fingers.

For the rest of the meal the guest has perfect service, and when he leaves, the maître d'hôtel says once more: 'So sorry about the soup,' and for this he gets sometimes one, two, or five dollars, but never from Mr Munsey.

Ludwig Bemelmans, *Hotel Bemelmans*, 1946

On a more flippant note, the following exchange is alleged to have taken place at the Queen's Hotel, Leeds, when two famous English cricketers booked in.

The England team had assembled at the Queen's Hotel in Leeds on the Wednesday afternoon before the match, but Alec Bedser and Jack Crapp were late arriving. Surrey had been playing Gloucestershire and they had travelled up to Leeds together. Jack went into the hotel first ahead of Alec and approached the girl receptionist who did not recognize him as one of the England team.

'Bed sir?', she said.

'No Crapp,' replied Jack, thinking she had mistaken him for Alec.

'Second door on the left,' said the receptionist as she returned to her books.

Brian Johnston, *It's Been a Lot of Fun*, 1974

Of course the opportunities for confusion are multiplied when one is having to cope with a foreign language. Miles Kington offers a language lesson in Franglais in this dialogue, 'Le Hotel Breakfast.'

GARÇON. Vous êtes prêt à choisir?

MONSIEUR. Je n'ai pas un menu.

GARÇON. Il n'y a pas un menu. Je fais une récitation des choses availables.

MONSIEUR. Alors, récitez. Je suis tout oreilles.

GARÇON. Il y a le breakfast continental à 95p ou le full English breakfast à £1.60.

MONSIEUR. En quoi ça consiste, le continental?

GARÇON. Toast, beurre, jam, thé ou café.

MONSIEUR. Toast et jam est trop exciting, trop foreign et daring pour moi. Dites-moi le breakfast full English.

GARÇON. Pour commencer, il y a des fruit juices ...

MONSIEUR. Des fruit juices anglais? Bon! Quelle sorte?

GARÇON. Eh bien, d'orange, de grapefruit, de tomates ...

MONSIEUR. Pas les oranges anglaises. Ce n'est pas la saison.

GARÇON. Il y a segments ...

MONSIEUR. Non, merci.

GARÇON. Ou des céreales. Il y a Rough-Brek, Ready-Shreds, Man-Made Fibres, Wholemeal Kleenex ou Timber-Bits. C'est fantastique pour les bowels.

MONSIEUR. Non, merci.

GARÇON. Pour continuer, il y a bacon, egg, sausage et tomatoes. Ou egg, bacon et sausage. Ou sausage et bacon. Ou n'importe quelle combinaison de toutes ces ingrédients. Avec chips extra.

MONSIEUR. Corrigez-moi si j'ai tort, mais c'est exactement la même chose que le full lunch anglais, en changeant son nom en 'mixed grill'.

GARÇON. Oui, monsieur.

MONSIEUR. Extraordinaire. Il n'y a pas une alternative?

GARÇON. Si, monsieur, Kippers.

MONSIEUR. Expliquez-moi ça.

GARÇON. C'est un petit animal qui consiste en 1,000 bones, brown dye et une odeur de poisson.

MONSIEUR. Non, merci.

GARÇON. Puis il y a toast, beurre, jam et thé ou café.

MONSIEUR. Ah? Après un full English on mange un continental breakfast?

GARÇON. C'est normal. On peut le manger aussi avec le high tea.

MONSIEUR. Extraordinaire.

GARÇON. Qu'est-ce qu'il va prendre, monsieur, alors?

MONSIEUR. Rien, merci. J'ai soudain perdu tout

appétit. Seulement une demi-bouteille de champagne et *The Times*.

GARÇON. Le bar n'est pas ouvert, monsieur, et *The Times* est closed.

MONSIEUR. Bon. Je pars.

GARÇON. Au revoir, monsieur.

Miles Kington, *Let's Parler Franglais*, 1979

An everyday occurrence in hotels is guests leaving things behind. John Fothergill has this story when he was landlord of the Spreadeagle, Thame.

There are two kinds of people who lose things: those who leave them in the place, go away and never know it – instead of being sorry for them and ultimately assimilating or throwing away their leavings, I suppose I ought to report the loss to the police. And for those who say they have left things and haven't I can't be sorry. But the other day I mixed the two kinds myself. Coming in from a walk I met on the steps a nice woman who had called for a hat that a friend said he had left behind. Not seeing any on the hooks, and Bessie denying that any hat had been left in a bed-room, I was rather irritated by her certainty, evident even through her politeness, of its being here, and I sent her off. But as soon as she was out of sight I found the hat on my head. I could think of only one clue towards tracing her or him. She had told me that the man had had a friend staying the week-end at Brill in a house where there was no bathroom, so I tele-phoned to the post-mistress there, who, after laughing merrily at this anguish-making incident, told me that in Brill *all* the houses had no bathrooms!

John Fothergill, *An Innkeeper's Diary*, 1931

On the subject of lost property, the last word should be given to James Thurber.

An article was found after your departure in the room which you occupied. Kindly let us know if you have

missed such an article, and if so, send us a description
and instructions as to what disposition you wish made
of same. For lack of space, all Lost and Found articles
must be disposed of within two months.

LOST AND FOUND DEPARTMENT
HOTEL LEXINGTON
Lexington Ave. & 48th St., New York
Per R. E. Daley.

Dear Mr Daley:

This whole thing is going to be much more complicated than you think. I have waited almost two weeks
before answering your postcard notification because I
have been unable to figure out what article I left
behind. I'm sorry now I didn't just forget the whole
business. As a matter of fact, I did try to forget it,
but it keeps bobbing up in my mind. I have got into
an alphabetical rut about it; at night I lie awake
naming articles to myself: bathrobe, bay rum, book,
bicycle, belt, baby, etc. Dr Prill, my analyst, has
advised me to come right out and meet you on the
subject.

So far, I have been able to eliminate, for certain,
only two articles. I never remember to take pyjamas
or a hairbrush with me, so it couldn't be pyjamas or
a hairbrush you found. This does not get us very far.
I have, however, ransacked the house and I find that a
number of things are missing, but I don't remember
which of them, if any, I had with me at the Lexington
that night: the vest to my blue suit, my life-insurance
policy, my Scotch terrier Jeannie, the jack out of the
automobile tool case, the bottle-opener that is supposed
to be kept in the kitchen drawer, the glass top to the
percolator, a box of aspirin, a letter from my father
giving my brother William's new address in Seattle, a
roll of films (exposed) for a 2A Kodak, my briefcase
(missing since 1927), etc. The article you have on hand
might be any of these (with the exception of the
briefcase). It would have been entirely possible for me,

[94]

in the state of mind I was in that Friday, to have gone about all day with the automobile jack in my hand.

The thing that worries me most is the possibility that what I left in my room was something the absence of which I have not yet discovered and may never discover, unless you give me some hint. Is it animal, vegetable, or mineral? Is it as big as I am? Twice as big? Smaller than a man's hand? Does it have a screw-on top? Does it make any kind of regular ticking noise when in operation? Is it worth, new, as much as a hundred dollars? A thousand dollars? Fifty cents? It isn't a bottle of toothache drops, is it? Or a used razor blade? Because I left them behind on purpose. These questions, it seems to me, are eminently fair. I'm not asking you some others I could think of, such as: Does it go with the pants and coat of a blue suit? Can it bark? Can it lift the wheel of an automobile off the ground? Can it open a bottle? Does it relieve pain? Is it a letter from somebody? Does anybody get any money out of it when I am dead, providing I keep the payments up?

I think you should let me know whether you are willing to answer yes or no to my first set of questions, as in all games of this sort. Because if you are just going to stand there with a silly look on your face and shake your head and keep repeating 'Can't guess what it i-yis, can't guess what it i-yis!' to hell with it. I don't care if it's a diamond ring.

I take it for granted, of course, that I really did leave an article in the room I occupied. If I didn't, and this thing turns out to be merely a guessing game in which the answer is Robert E. Lee's horse, or something, you'll never be able to answer your phone for a whole year without running the chance of it's being me, reserving dozens of rooms in a disguised voice and under various assumed names, reporting a fire on the twenty-third floor, notifying you that your bank balance is overdrawn, pretending, in a husky guttural, that you are the next man the gang is going to put on the spot for the shooting of Joe the Boss over in Brooklyn.

Of course, I'm a little sore about the thing the way it is. If you had been a guest at my house and had gone away leaving your watch or your keyring behind, would I send you a penny postcard asking you to guess what you had left behind? I would now, yes; but I mean before this all happened. Supposing everybody did business that way. Supposing your rich and doting uncle wired you: 'I'm arriving Grand Central some time next month. Meet me.' Or, worse yet, supposing that instead of issuing a summons naming a definite crime or misdemeanour, the courts sent out a postcard reading: 'I know what's going to happen to you-oo!' We'd all be nervous wrecks.

The only thing I see to do right now is comply with your request for a description of the article I left in that room. It is a large and cumbersome iron object, usually kept in a kitchen drawer, entitling my wife, upon my death, to a certain payment of money; it barks when in operation and, unless used when the coffee reaches the boiling point, will allow the liquid to spill out on the stove; it is signed by my father's name, is sensitive to light, relieves neuralgic pains, and is dark blue in colour.

James Thurber, *Vintage Thurber*, 1963

Travel writers love to tell of the fortunes and tribu-
lations they meet along the road. In the late sixteenth
century, Montaigne and his secretary were en route
from Venice to Rome. Here the secretary describes his
master's enjoyment of the precursors of the modern
hotel touts.

He took all possible delight in the rivalry between the
landlords. They have a custom of sending seven or
eight leagues to meet strangers to implore them to
choose their inn. You will often meet the landlord
himself on horseback and in various places several well-
dressed men are on the watch for you. All along the
road he amused himself by humouring them and
listening to the various offers made by each. There is
nothing they will not promise (someone, probably
Montaigne himself, has added in the margin '*anche
ragazze e ragazzi*', 'even girls and boys'). There was
one who offered him a hare purely as a gift if he
would only inspect his house. Their disputes and
rivalry stop at the gates of the town and they do not
venture to say a word more. They have it in common
that they offer you a guide on horseback, at their
own expense, to guide you and carry part of your
baggage to the inn you are going to; which they
always do and pay the expense. I do not know whether
they are obliged to do this by some regulation, because
of the danger of the roads.

We had made our bargain before we left Bologna
for what we had to pay and get in return at Lojano,
being strongly advised to do so by the people of the
inn where we stayed. So he had sent one of us to
inspect all the inns, the provisions and wines, and

learn the conditions before dismounting, and he chose the best. But it is impossible to make such careful terms that you escape their trickery; for they will keep you short of wood, candles, linen, or they will fail to supply the hay which you have omitted to specify.

Diary of Montaigne's Journey to Italy,
late sixteenth century

In the nineteenth century, many hotels were built in the wake of the great railway boom. Dickens wrote these notes on railway hotels in 1859, but his observations are as relevant today as they were 125 years ago. His final sentence, in particular, will strike echoes with many readers: most hotels these days are 'largely wholesale', and there is still that 'lingering personal retail interest that asks to be satisfied'.

We all know the new hotel near the station, where it is always gusty, going up the lane which is always muddy, where we are sure to arrive at night, and where we make the gas start awfully when we open the front door. We all know the flooring of the passages and staircases that is too new, and the walls that are too new, and the house that is haunted by the ghost of mortar. We all know the doors that have cracked, and the cracked shutters through which we get a glimpse of the disconsolate moon. We all know the new people, who have come to keep the new hotel, and who wish they had never come, and who (inevitable result) wish *we* had never come. We all know how much too scant and smooth and bright the new furniture is, and how it has never settled down, and cannot fit itself into right places, and will get into wrong places. We all know how the gas, being lighted, shows maps of Damp upon the walls. We all know how the ghost of mortar passes into our sandwich, stirs our negus, goes up to bed with us, ascends the pale bedroom chimney, and prevents the smoke from following. We all know how a leg of our chair comes off at breakfast in the morning, and how the dejected waiter attributes the accident to a general greenness pervading the establishment, and informs us, in reply to a local inquiry, that he is thankful to say he is an entire stranger in that part of the country, and is going back to his own connexion on Saturday.

We all know, on the other hand, the great station hotel belonging to the company of proprietors, which has suddenly sprung up in the back outskirts of any place we like to name, and where we look out of our palatial windows, at little back yards and gardens, old summer-houses, fowl-houses, pigeon-traps, and pigsties. We all know this hotel in which we can get anything we want, after its kind, for money; but where nobody is glad to see us, or sorry to see us, or minds (our bill paid) whether we come or go, or how, or when, or why, or cares about us. We all know this hotel, where we have no individuality, but put ourselves into the general post, as it were, and are sorted and disposed of according to our division. We all know that we can get on very well indeed at such a place, but still not perfectly well; and this may be, because the place is largely wholesale, and there is a lingering, personal retail interest within us that asks to be satisfied.

Charles Dickens, *The Uncommercial Traveller*, 1859

*Cook's Tours became increasingly popular as the nine-
teenth century drew towards its close, and changed
the character of many hotels. Here is an early comment
on Thomas Cook.*

The hotel Bellevue, which looks upon the sea and
hears always the waves dashing upon the worn and
jagged rocks, was overflowed by one of those swarms,
which are the nuisance of independent travelers,
known as a 'Cook's Party', excellent people individually
no doubt, but monopolizing hotels and steamboats, and
driving everybody else into obscurity by reason of
their numbers and compact organization. We passed
yesterday one of the places on the coast where Jonah
is said to have left the whale; it is suspected – though
without any contemporary authority – that he was
in a Cook's Party of his day, and left it in disgust for
this private conveyance.

Charles Dudley Warner, *In the Levant*, 1876

*After the railways came the aeroplane and the age of
cheap travel. The packaging of tourists has become
global big business. D. J. Enright commemorates the
new kind of hotel user in his poem 'Tourist Promotion'.*

For the tourists, who stay in the
Large new tourist hotels, the
Chief tourist attractions are the
Other large new tourist hotels.

For the querulous and wayward
There were once the local monkeys.
Who lived in the ancient tree-tops
Long before the hotels were thought of.
The tourists enticed the monkeys down
From the trees with monkey nuts and
Breakfast rolls. And the monkeys
Scampered across the road and were
Squashed by the buses transporting
Fresh tourists to see the monkeys.
It was not a pretty sight.

So now the tourists are confined to
The tourist hotels, large and new.
They pass with the greatest of ease
From one to the other, escorted by porters
With large new umbrellas, or even through
Underground passages, air-conditioned and
Adorned with murals by local artists
Conveying impressions of the local scene.
After all, the tourist hotels were created
Specifically for the sake of the tourists.

D. J. Enright, *Collected Poems*, 1981

One of the risks you run when you arrive at a new hotel is to find that not everything is working as it should. Of course such hazards also exist in old hotels, but not in quite the same way. Sybille Bedford describes her visit to the newly-opened Hotel Guzman in Guadalajara in Mexico.

We pulled up in front of a large and beautiful six-teenth-century palace. 'Hotel Guzman,' said Anthony. 'Don't worry, it's all fixed up new inside. You've never seen such bathrooms. Solid black marble.'

We all shot up in a small, fast lift. The manager flung open a door and ushered us into a splendid apartment full of divan beds and somebody's clothes.

'Why that's *my* room,' said Anthony.

'Yes, Sir. I had beds for the ladies moved in while you were absent.'

'Now, see here . . . ' said Anthony.

E. took over. 'We do not want to be three in a room,' she said gently.

'No room for three? But the gentleman said he was expecting two ladies.'

'Yes, and here we are. But you see we don't want all three to share one room.'

'That is all right, Señora. It is a large room. In Holy Week when there are many travellers we would have a family of seven, nine persons in such a room. And their servants in the bathroom.'

'But this isn't Holy Week.'

'It is not, Señora. In Holy Week there would be a family and servants in every room, now it is only one gentleman and two ladies. It costs more in Holy Week, too.'

'Look here,' I said, 'we have strange habits and we want two, or at least one other room. Have you got them?'

'Yes, yes, many rooms. We are the newest hotel in Guadalajara.'

'Well, can we see them?'

'They are very new, Señora. More new than this room. We are still working on the newness.'

After a good deal more of this, a bed for Anthony was moved into a cupboard leading out of our room. The cupboard had a window, but it opened into a corridor. Ours had an open view over red-tiled roof tops and a brilliant nocturnal sky. The night was warmer than it had been in Morelia. We were very hungry.

A cry of distress from E. in the bathroom. 'My dear, I can't make the water run. Do try.'

Indeed: hot tap, cold tap, tub and basin, not a drop. There was a telephone on the wall, I picked it up.

'There doesn't seem to be any water in our bathroom.'

'Of course not, Señora. It has not been laid on. One thing after another. Perhaps next year? Yes, certainly next year. If we do well. You will recommend us?'

Ready first, I proceeded to go downstairs. I walked up the corridor, none too well-lit, then saw, caught myself, and knees buckling reeled a step backward, collapsed against a wall and howled for Anthony.

He came running. 'What's the matter?'

'Anthony, THERE ARE NO STAIRS.'

'Well, what d'you want stairs for?'

'I was about to go down.'

'What's wrong with the elevator?'

'Oh God, Anthony, don't be so yourself. And don't

let's have a Mexican conversation. Go and see ... No, don't go! Be careful!'

Anthony went a few steps up the corridor. 'Jesus Christ,' he said.

The corridor ended in space. Seventy feet below, at the bottom of the crater left by flights of marble recently ripped out, lay invisible in a dim pool of light the reception desk, the leather armchairs and the spittoons of the entrance hall. Between, a void. They had begun working on the newness on the top floor. Anthony and I fetched E. from the room and we all went down in the lift.

> Sybille Bedford, *A Visit to Don Otavio.*
> *A Mexican Journey*, 1982

Smollett complains of the sanitary arrangements in Nîmes in 1763 – even worse than Scotland:

Provence is a pleasant country, well cultivated; but the inns are not so good here as in Languedoc, and few of them are provided with a certain convenience which an English traveller can very ill dispense with. Those you find are generally on the tops of houses, exceedingly nasty; and so much exposed to the weather, that a valetudinarian cannot use them without hazard of his life. At Nismes in Languedoc, where we found the temple of Cloacina (the goddess of sewers) in a most shocking condition, the servant-maid told me her mistress had caused it to be made on purpose for the English travellers; but now she was very sorry for what she had done, as all the French who frequented her house, instead of using the seat, left their offerings on the floor, which she was obliged to have cleaned three or four times a day. This is a degree of beastliness, which would appear detestable even in the capital of North-Britain.

Tobias Smollett, *Travels through France and Italy*, 1763

In 1935 Italy invaded Abyssinia. Evelyn Waugh was sent out as a war correspondent. Here is his description of how one of Addis Ababa's chief hotels faced its finest hour.

There were several hotels in Addis Ababa, all, at the time of our arrival, outrageously prosperous. 'Kakophilos's,' at which we all assumed we should stay, was completely full with journalists and photographers living in hideous proximity, two or three to a room even in the outbuildings. It was a massive, shabby building of sepulchral gloom, presided over by the eponymous, sturdy, middle-aged, misanthropic Greek, who had taken it over as a failing concern just before the troubles. There was something admirable about the undisguised and unaffected distaste with which he regarded his guests and his ruthless disregard of their comfort and dignity. Some attempted to be patronising to him, some dictatorial, some ingratiating; all were treated with uniform contempt. He was well aware that for a very few months nothing that he did or left undone could affect his roaring prosperity; after that anything might happen. The less his guests ate the greater his profits, and from his untidy little desk in the corner he watched with sardonic amusement the crowds of dyspeptic journalists – many of them elderly men, of note in their own countries – furtively carrying into his dining-room paper bags of fresh bread, tins of tuck and pocketfuls of oranges and bananas, like little boys trooping into tea at their private schools.

Mr Kakophilos never apologised and very rarely complained. Nothing of the smallest value was endangered in the scenes of violence which became increasingly frequent as the journalists made themselves at home. When his guests threw their bedroom furniture out of the window, he noted it in the weekly bill. If they fired their revolvers at the night watchman he merely advised the man to take careful cover. Menageries of unclean pets were introduced into the bedrooms; Mr Kakophilos waited unconcerned until even their owners could bear their presence no longer. His was the chief hotel of the town and nothing could shake its status.

Evelyn Waugh, *When the Going Was Good*, 1946

Hotels adapt themselves in different ways to crises. James Cameron visited the Himalaya Hotel in Kalimpong during a time of mass invasion of the town by Tibetan refugees.

The Himalaya Hotel is a commonplace name for a most exceptional place. If I keep so persistently harping on hotels it is only that, having spent quite a disproportionate part of my life in them, I have come to classify and record them much as, I believe, accomplished winelovers define clarets, less for their appearance and cost as for their associations and bouquet. The Himalaya was, by those standards, a collector's piece. It was (and I hope still is) the nearest thing to what I imagine the seventeenth-century English inn must have been, in its broad-minded and casual attitude to the one factor absent from almost all other hotels, hospitality. People came in, and drifted about, and occupied themselves with erratic pursuits, and told incredible stories in several languages, and made abrupt appearances in extravagant clothes, and no one was there an hour before he would find himself involved and embraced in the inescapable community life of the place. Which was all the odder since the place was full of those most exclusive and (as we always imagined) unclubbable of all peoples, Tibetans.

That night I bathed in a large tin tub and went into what in any other hotel would have been called a lounge, for what anywhere else would have been called a quick drink, before what in most other places would have been dinner. In no single particular was this purpose accomplished; rather, in every aspect did it materialize some ten times life-size. To call this room a lounge would have been ridiculous; it was a salon, a caravanserai, a large room crowded, as we saw with surprise, with a multitude of striking and picturesque people in richly-coloured costume and exceptional hairdressings; they were occupied not, as one might have thought, in being photographed for the *National Geographical Magazine*, but in a variety of pleasantly domestic occupations such as pouring tots of rum and knitting socks, and discussing questions of mutual interest in an animated and formal way. Most of them were Tibetans; there were also several people who might have been economics lecturers on vacation, refugees from Cheltenham Ladies' College, and at least one who was quite evidently a Benedictine monk in disguise. Before our entry we had considered dubiously whether our appearances – unshaven, khaki-shirted, carpet-slippered – might have been thought indecorous. We need not have worried.

We were received with a courtesy that was almost enthusiastic. The hostess, Mrs Annie Perry, said: 'Now do come in and meet some lovely people; I know you won't mind joining us, it just happens we were having a little party tonight.' (It turned out later that one would require to be singularly out of luck to arrive at the Himalaya, at any day of the year, when this was not the case.) 'Now sit down somewhere, and what will you have; it so happens there's only rum. You must talk to this dear lady; I know you'll want to meet her; she has come a great distance.'

This was a Tibetan lady of high degree, attired most gaily in a dark blue smock with the traditional apron of vivid horizontal candy-stripes, high felt boots and gold earrings; she made a place beside me on a divan and said, in impeccable English and with a grave interest: 'You come all the way from England.'

Then I realized that values had to be changed.

The character of that evening – unremarkable, simple, possibly commonplace in such surroundings – has ever since been hard to convey; an atmosphere both grotesque and elusive; certainly unforgettable.

James Cameron, *Point of Departure*, 1967

Bruce Chatwin meets unexpected generosity in a hotel in Patagonia.

The hotel in Rio Pico was painted a pale turquoise and run by a Jewish family who lacked even the most elementary notions of profit. The rooms shambled round a courtyard with a water-tower and flower-beds edged with upturned bottles and full of fierce orange lilies. The owner was a brave and sorrowful woman in black, with heavy-lidded eyes, mourning with a Jewish mother's passion the death of her first-born son. He had been a saxophonist. He had gone to Comodoro Rivadavia and died there, of stomach cancer. She picked her teeth with a thorn and laughed at the futility of existence.

Her second son, Carlos Rubén, was an olive-skinned boy with the flickering eyes of a Semite. He ached for the outside world and would soon disappear into it. Her daughters padded the bare scrubbed rooms in carpet slippers. She ordered a towel and a pink geranium to be put in my room.

In the morning I had a tremendous row about the bill.

'How much was the room?'

'Nothing. If you hadn't slept in it, nobody else would.'

'How much was dinner?'

'Nothing. How could we know you were coming? We cooked for ourselves.'

'Then how much was the wine?'

'We always give wine to visitors.'

'What about the maté?'

'Nobody pays for maté.'

'What can I pay for then? There's only bread and coffee left.'

'I can't charge you for bread, but café au lait is a gringo drink and I shall make you pay.'

Bruce Chatwin, *In Patagonia*, 1977

We end as we began, with an inn as a haven of delight. George Mikes finds a curious contentment at a traditional Japanese ryokan.

You will – or anyway you should – stay a few days in a *ryokan*, a Japanese inn. They are usually beautiful and well-run and there you can get closer to real Japanese life than almost anywhere else.

You arrive, say, at five p.m. and you get your first dinner early. Pretty, smiling waitresses in *kimonos* will bring in your meal on a tray. You sit on the *tatami*, the exquisitely woven straw-mat, on the floor, wearing your *yukata* and feel that you look like a minor official of the Tokugawa period.

You finish your dinner, the charming lady – more a hostess than a maid – will come in and within five minutes will transform your room. It will be a complete change of scenery – and scenery is the right word because the whole set-up is slightly yet pleasantly theatrical. The little low table will disappear on to the balcony, two mattresses will be laid out on the *tatami*, one covered with a red, the other with a blue eiderdown. A jug of iced water is placed next to your pillow and a small, weak foot-light is left on, near the door.

Next morning the scene is changed back: the mattresses disappear and you are delighted with your pretty room until you realise, after lunch, that you cannot lie down anywhere even for ten minutes. Your mattresses are neatly stored in the cupboard and there is just nothing to lie on unless, of course, you lie down on the bare *tatami* – the English equivalent of which would be to put your knife into your mouth and scratch your head with your fork.

The *tatami* is sacred. You will be initiated into the shoe-ceremony on your arrival. On coming home, you take your shoes off and the porter takes charge of them and keeps them for you in his little hut. You step into a pair of lovely, comfortable slippers, always placed in such a way that you should be able to slip your feet straight into them, without touching them with your hands. You use these slippers everywhere in the house, except ... except that you must also learn the loo-ceremony. When going to the loo you step out of your ordinary slippers and step into the special loo-slippers, and leaving that establishment you leave the loo-slippers facing the entrance so that the next visitor – probably yourself – will be able to step into them without touching them with his hands. This is regarded as elementary courtesy to yourself. You have also to learn the *tatami*-ceremony: before stepping on the *tatami* you must take your slippers off. There are no special slippers for the *tatami*: you must walk on it in your stockinged feet. The most heinous crime, of course, is to walk on the *tatami* wearing your loo-slippers; a crime which – being thoroughly confused by all this changing of slippers – you frequently commit.

You really feel at home in the *ryokan*. They are sweet to you, charming and welcoming. As soon as you come home – and you may return home ten times a day – your own maid will bring you hot towels – a very refreshing and civilised habit – and a pot of green tea which most people love but I detest. The Japanese are as sensitive about their tea as the English, so I invariably poured my tea down the loo (usually wearing my non-loo slippers) because they would have been hurt if I had just left it. The loo itself in my *ryokan* was a Western one with sketches and drawings and written instructions in Japanese, meant for absolute beginners, on how to use it. (The drawings were very neat, showing a gentleman in standing and sitting position, and the text, I was told, was concise and instructive, composed by the Professor of Scatology, Tokyo University.)

Soon afterwards I discovered an admirable institution, common to all *ryokans*. Our maid came in with a roneod booklet of Japanese phrases, the English translation written next to them. She pointed to the English question: 'What do you want for breakfast?' I pointed to the Japanese answer: 'Coffee, toast and boiled egg.' She asked with her fingers: 'At what time?' 'Eight thirty,' I pointed, in fluent Japanese.

The little booklet caused one of the bitterest disappointments of my life. One day my pretty maid, wearing her alluring *kimono*, came in and pointed to the question: 'Do you want to see my front?'

I nodded. Yes, I would be very pleased to see her front.

She pointed: 'Please follow me.'

I followed her, not a little surprised and with an air of anticipation. But all she wanted was for me to see her front desk.

The *ryokan* closed its doors at 12 p.m. and there was a large and conspicuous sign at the entrance, in English:

'ALL GUESTS ARE REQUESTED TO BE
UNITED IN BED BEFORE MIDNIGHT'

That was the clearest and most lucid instruction I ever came across in Japan.

George Mikes, *The Land of the Rising Yen*, 1970

꧁꧂

Acknowledgements

꧁꧂

An anthologist writing his acknowledgements is like a bridegroom making his wedding speech: he knows that there are innumerable people to thank and that he is sure to forget several key names. Norman Brangham, Derek Cooper, Christopher Driver, John J. Grenz, Bevis Hillier, Diane Latham, J. G. Links, Kenneth McLeish, Jan Morris, Caroline Raphael, and Richard Usborne have all contributed valuable suggestions, but I know that there are many others who, during the course of the book's preparation, have pointed me in fruitful directions. May I thank both the named and the unnamed, and will the latter please forgive me for a faulty memory?

The editor and publishers gratefully acknowledge permission to use the following copyright material:

Sue Arnold: *Glutton-backed Chairs and Cherubs* from *The Observer*, © 1981 The Observer Ltd. By permission.

Sybille Bedford: From *A Visit to Don Otavio. A Mexican Journey* (Eland Books, 1982). First published under the title *The Sudden View* by Victor Gollancz Ltd., 1953. Reprinted by permission of the author.

Lucius Beebe: *The Savoy of London*. Copyright Holiday Magazine, 1953. Reprinted by permission of Travel-Holiday, Floral Park, New York.

Hilaire Belloc: 'Tarantella' from *Complete Verse*. Copyright © 1970 The Estate of Hilaire Belloc. Reprinted by permission of Gerald Duckworth & Co. Ltd., and A. D. Peters & Co. Ltd.

Ludwig Bemelmans: From *Hotel Bemelmans* (Viking, 1946). Reprinted by permission of Madeleine Bemelmans, Executrix for the Estate of Ludwig Bemelmans.

John Betjeman: 'The Arrest of Oscar Wilde at the Cadogan Hotel' from *Collected Poems* (4th revised edn., 1979). Reprinted by permission of John Murray (Publishers) Ltd.

John Burke: From *The English Inn* (1981). Reprinted by permission of B. T. Batsford Ltd.

James Cameron: From *Point of Departure* (Weidenfeld, 1967). Copyright © James Cameron 1967. Reprinted by permission of David Higham Associates Ltd.

Casanova: From *History of My Life*, Vol. 9, trans. Willard R. Trask (1970). Copyright © 1970 by Harcourt Brace Jovanovich, Inc. Reprinted by permission of Penguin Books Ltd., and Harcourt Brace Jovanovich, Inc.

Bruce Chatwin: From *In Patagonia* (1977). Copyright © 1977 by Bruce Chatwin. Reprinted by permission of Jonathan Cape Ltd., and Simon & Schuster, Inc., for the author.

John Cleese and Connie Booth: From *Fawlty Towers* (Contact Publications, 1979). Copyright © 1979 John Cleese and Connie Booth. Reprinted by permission of David Wilkinson Associates.

Warwick Deeping: From *Sorrell and Son* (Cassell, 1921).

Reprinted by permission of Macmillan Publishing Company, New York.

Anne Edwards and Steven Citron: From *The Inn and Us* (1976). Copyright © 1976 by Anne Edwards and Steven Citron. Reprinted by permission of Random House, Inc., and International Creative Management for the authors.

D. J. Enright: 'Tourist Promotion' from *Collected Poems* (OUP, 1981). Reprinted by permission of Watson, Little Ltd., for the author.

John Fothergill: From *An Innkeeper's Diary* (1931). Reprinted by permission of Chatto & Windus Ltd., and the author's Literary Estate.

Russell Harty: *Hols at the Hotel Tralee* from *The Observer*. Copyright © 1980 The Observer Ltd. By permission.

John Irving: From *The World According to Garp* (Gollancz/Dutton, 1978). Copyright © 1976, 1977, 1978 by John Irving. Reprinted by permission of A. D. Peters Ltd.

Brian Johnston: From *It's Been a Lot of Fun* (1974). Reprinted by permission of W. H. Allen & Co., Ltd.

Miles Kington: From *Let's Parler Franglais* (1979). Reprinted by permission of Robson Books Ltd.

Patrick Leigh-Fermor: From *A Time of Gifts* (1977). Reprinted by permission of John Murray (Publishers) Ltd.

George Mikes: From *The Land of the Rising Yen* (1970). Reprinted by permission of André Deutsch Ltd.

Eric Newby: From *Slowly Down the Ganges* (Picador, 1983). Reprinted by permission of the author.

George Orwell: From *Down and Out in Paris and London*. Copyright 1933 by George Orwell, renewed 1961 by Sonia Pitt-Rivers. Reprinted by permission of Harcourt Brace Jovanovich, Inc., and A. M. Heath Ltd., for the Estate of the late Sonia Brownell and Martin Secker & Warburg, Ltd.

S. J. Perelman: From *Westward Ha!* and *Acres and Pains*. Copyright © 1930, 1958 by S. J. Perelman, collected in *The Most of S. J. Perelman* (Wm. Heinemann Ltd/Simon & Schuster, Inc.). Reprinted by permission of A. D. Peters & Co. Ltd., and Simon & Schuster, Inc.

Jonathan Raban: From *Arabia Through the Looking Glass* (Collins, 1979; published in America by Simon & Schuster under the title *Arabia: A Journey Through the Labyrinth*, 1979). Reprinted by permission of William Collins Sons & Co., Ltd., and Gillon Aitken for the author.

Marie Louise Ritz: From *César Ritz* (1938). Reprinted by permission of Harrap Ltd.

Halliday Sutherland: From *A Hebridean Journey* (Geoffrey Bles, 1939).

Studs Terkel: From *Working: People Talk About What They Do All Day and How They Feel About What They Do*. Copyright © 1972, 1974 by Studs Terkel. Reprinted by permission of Pantheon Books, a Division of Random House, Inc., and Wildwood House Ltd.

D. M. Thomas: From *The White Hotel*. Copyright © 1981 by D. M. Thomas. Reprinted by permission of Victor Gollancz Ltd., and Viking Penguin Inc.

James Thurber: From *The Middle-Aged Man on the Flying Trapeze*, published by Harper & Row, copyright 1935 James Thurber, copyright © 1963 Helen W. Thurber and Rosemary T. Sauers; collected in *Vintage Thurber*, edited by Helen Thurber, Vol. 2. Copyright © 1963 Hamish Hamilton Ltd.

ACKNOWLEDGEMENTS

Reprinted by permission of Mrs James Thurber and Hamish Hamilton Ltd.

John K. Walton: From *The Blackpool Landlady* (1978). Reprinted by permission of Manchester University Press.

Christopher Wiseman: 'Hotel Dining Room, London' from *The Upper Hand* (1981). Reprinted by permission of Enitharmon Press for the author.

P. G. Wodehouse: From *Full Moon* (Barry & Jenkins, Ltd., 1947). Reprinted by permission of A. P. Watt Ltd. on behalf of Lady Ethel Wodehouse, and Scott Meredith Literary Agency.

While every effort has been made to secure permission, we may have failed in a few cases to trace the copyright holder. We apologize for any apparent negligence.

The illustrations in this book were taken from the following sources: Jean-Anthelme Brillat-Savarin, *La Physiologie du Goût* (1825); Richard Doyle, *The Foreign Tour of Brown, Jones and Robinson* (London, 1854); Richard Doyle, from *Punch* (1849); Charles G. Harper, *The Old Inns of Old England*, 2 vols. (London, 1906); Clarence P. Hornung, *Handbook of Early Advertising Art* (New York, 1956); Stephen Lister, *Fit for a Bishop*, with illustrations by Val Biro (London, 1955) (Reprinted by permission of William Heinemann Limited); Irving Zucker, *A Source Book of French Advertising Art* (London, 1970).

Index